T0306760

ON THE ROAD city
Moscow

ON THE ROAD
Editor of collection
Laura Andreini

editorial project
Forma Edizioni srl, Firenze, Italia
redazione@formaedizioni.it
www.formaedizioni.it

editorial production
Archea Associati

editorial direction
Laura Andreini

textual supervision
Riccardo Bruscagli

authors
Alessandro De Magistris
Umberto Zanetti

editorial staff
Valentina Muscedra
Maria Giulia Caliri

graphic design
Elisa Balducci
Alberto Bolzonetti
Vitoria Muzi
Isabella Peruzzi
Mauro Sampaolesi

translations
Maureen Fay Young

photolithography
LAB di Gallotti Giuseppe Fulvio,
Firenze, Italia

printing
Gutenberg Press Limited,
Gudja Road, Tarxien, Malta
PLA 19

we would like to thank
Riccardo Crenna
Simona Flacco
Alessandra Dall'Ara
Yulia Filatova
Lorenza Bonamore
Giulia Arduini
for their collaboration

First Edition: April 2017

ISBN 978-88-96780-96-1

With the support of:

КОМИТЕТ ПО АРХИТЕКТУРЕ
И ГРАДОСТРОИТЕЛЬСТВУ
ГОРОДА МОСКВЫ

Moscow Committee for Architecture and Urban Development

АРХСОВЕТ
МОСКВЫ

Archcouncil of Moscow

MA

Schusev State Museum of Architecture

Table of contents

Guidebook as tool

On the Road is a new collection of contemporary architecture guidebooks whose purpose is to tell about a place, whether a city or larger area, through its architectural works chosen to be visited and experienced directly.

The guidebook has a convenient special jacket that opens into a map marking the location of the architectural works and interesting sites to visit. On the back are miniature images and addresses of the architectural works described in detail within.

The book starts with short essays explaining the city or area's present day and history and outlining possible future scenarios with planned or imminent projects. Each work features of a photograph of the whole, an architectural drawing (plan or section), a short description, and facts including architect, type, year of construction, address, website, and how to visit it.

The finest architecture of each city and suggested routes are represented by this collection of not-to-be-missed, "timeless" buildings that uniquely define their settings. General information and useful tips for travelers help them optimize their visits and quickly understand the essence of the place described.

Museums, theatres, restaurants, hotels and a list of top architectural firms working in the city let visitors turn a regular trip into an opportunity for study or work.

Note: The need to provide as complete a historical-architectural outline as possible led to the selection of over 100 buildings worth visiting. The opening list to each itinerary contains comprehensive descriptions of the buildings with detailed data sheets printed in bold type.

Key

00 architecture including detailed data sheet

(00) architecture without detailed data sheet

Moscow

Laura Andreini*

The On the Road series was created for an audience made up of not only architects but also curious travelers and enthusiasts who want a useful tool (in paper or app form) for visiting the world's great cities. We could not have failed to include Moscow, with its dynamic output of new works, both built and under construction.

Moscow is studded with cyclical changes to its urban fabric, imposed by corresponding social and political changes: the demands of a tsar, breaks with the past dictated by revolutions, or the resolute measures of the communist regime. The history and conformation of Moscow have made it the capital of an Eastern Europe with whom it shares a common heritage, that is the communist political system and all of its consequences, not least of which the Soviet model of urban planning. Now that the Soviet era has come to an end, Moscow remains the symbol of the rapid changes that all of these cities are facing today, albeit on different scales depending on their size and importance.

Moscow's ongoing process of urban modernization is taking its cues mainly from the experiences of the great cities of the world, in particular those in the West. At first, changes as rapid and rudderless as the new economy itself resulted mainly in forms that broke squarely with local traditions, for example the new Moscow City district, which is currently in the final phases of construction. Today, however, urban regeneration projects are increasingly oriented towards creating continuity with the wide open spaces and the vast industrial districts that are a legacy of the Soviet era. To address the transformation that is taking place, international competitions have been held with the involvement of important local and foreign architecture firms, for instance for the adaptation of the Serp i Molot and ZiL factories and for the reconstruction of Moscow's urban riverfronts.

In this way, the Russian capital has already begun to reveal what it intends to accomplish: the revitalization of the city's decrepit and abandoned industrial zones, the redevelopment of its vast urban voids, the reorganization of public transport to meet the changing needs of the population, and the realization of far-reaching projects assigned by means of international competitions.

* Architect and Associate Professor. Teaches and researches at the DIDA of Florence and works at Studio Archea of which she is co-founder; writer and Deputy Editor-in-Chief for *Area* magazine.

Political / geographical facts

country
Russia

language
Russian

area code
+7 (495) or (499)

coordinates
55°45' 06" N
37°37' 04" E

area
2 561,5 sq.km

population
12.330.126

density
4.813,63 inhabitants / sq.km

time zone
UTC+3

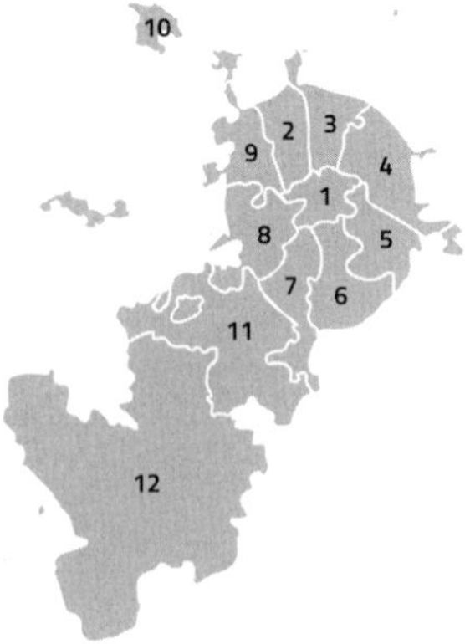

Administrative districts

1. Central
2. Northern
3. North-Eastern
4. Eastern
5. South-Eastern
6. Southern
7. South-Western
8. Western
9. North-Western
10. Zelenogradsky
11. Novomoskovsky
12. Troitsky

General information
useful addresses and numbers

WEBSITES AND MAIN OFFICES

Federal Agency for Tourism (Russiatourism)
http://www.russiatourism.ru/en/
Myasnitskaya ulitsa 47, 101000 Moscow
Mon -Thu / 9 am - 6 pm
Fri / 9 am - 4.45 pm

Moscow tourism portal
http://en.travel2moscow.com
Call center 8 800 220 0001 (from a local landline)
+7 800 220 0001 (from a foreign landline)

Official website of the City of Moscow
https://www.mos.ru/en/

EMERGENCY SERVICES

Police 02
Ambulance 03
Fire Department 01

URBAN TRANSPORT

Useful information on the city's transport systems and the purchasing and pricing of tickets and passes is available at the site http://www.expat.ru/s_transport.php
The site http://msk.rusavtobus.ru/en/ will help you decide the best means of transport to use based on your starting and destination points

Airport-city
Express trains take about 50 minutes between the Sheremetevo, Domodedovo, and Vnukovo airports and the Belorusskaya, Paveleskaya, and Kievskaya metro stations, respectively.
Tickets can be purchased at the departure points and on line
http://www.aeroexpress.ru/

Subway
Official site of the Moscow Metro
http://mosmetro.ru/
An interactive map is available on the site
http://engl.mosmetro.ru/flash/scheme01.html
The iPhone app can be found at
https://itunes.apple.com/it/app/metro-di-mosca/id476323439?mt=8

Bicycle rentals
Velobike
Service available from May through October
http://velobike.ru/

Car sharing
Belkacar.ru
Paveletskaya naberezhnaya 2, 115114 Moscow
Tel +7 (495) 234 3300
support@belkacar.ru

GENERAL CONSULATE OF FRANCE
Bolshaya Yakimanka 45, 115127 Moscow
Tel +7 (495) 937 1500

GENERAL CONSULATE OF GERMANY
Leninski prospekt 95A, 119313 Moscow
Tel +7 (495) 933 4311

GENERAL CONSULATE OF GREAT BRITAIN
Consular Services
Smolenskaya naberezhnaya 10, 121099 Moscow
Tel +7 (495) 956 7200

GENERAL CONSULATE OF ITALY
Yakimanskaya naberezhnaya 10, 119180 Moscow
Tel +7 (495) 796 9692

GENERAL CONSULATE OF SPAIN
Bolshaya Nikitskaya ulitsa 50/8, 121069 Moscow
Tel +7 (495) 202 2657

GENERAL CONSULATE OF THE UNITED STATES
ACS, U.S. Embassy Moscow
American Citizen Services
21 Novinskiy Bulvar 21, 123242 Moscow
Tel +7 (495) 728 5577

HOW TO PHONE

From a local landline: dial the trunk prefix 8, then the city prefix (495 or 499), then the number

From a foreign landline: dial international prefix (+7), city prefix (495 or 499) and the number

Useful tips

1. Getting around_For long and medium distances, the vast **Metro** network is the best way to travel. You can avoid lines at the stations and save money overall by purchasing smart cards with journey credits or travel passes that allow unlimited travel.
Outside of the historic Boulevard Ring, the early twentieth-century perimeter of the city, it can be pleasant to use the surface transport, in particular **trams**, **buses**, and **trolleybuses**, especially in summertime.
While there are still only a limited number of bicycle paths, **cycle hire** is an excellent way to travel along the tree-lined Bulvar.
Because of chronic traffic congestion, it is best to avoid using private cars, except on weekends, when Moscovites all escape to their dachas.
Taxis can be found at airports, rail terminals and some metro stations. Book several hours ahead of time by phone or online if you want to be picked up from a specific place. Companies like Uber or Get-a-Taxi have handy mobile apps for booking rides within minutes.
Also available in Moscow are informal "taxi" services consisting of private citizens circulating the city in their own car and offering rides. They can be flagged on the street by holding out your arm. The fare must be negotiated before the start of the trip and will almost always take place in Russian. The inexperienced are not advised to use this method of transport. A **car sharing** service is also available. For information see the website Belkacar.ru.

2. Eating_To keep food costs down, you can eat at kiosk chains like Kroshka-Kartoshka, Teremok, or Riksha Ivan, and Russian restaurant chains like Mu-Mu, Elki-Palki, or Grabli. Also worth trying are Stolovaya 57 (the reconstruction of a typical Soviet canteen), located inside the GUM department store, or, if you can pass as a student, the university cafeterias, in particular the one at MGU.

3. Sleeping_In alternative to more refined solutions, you can stay at an international hotel chain, such as Holiday Inn, Mercure, or Ibis. Book early because the prices can rise sharply in certain times of the year, even at these types of hotels.

4. Must-see highlights_Sites that should not be missed include the Red Square and the adjacent GUM department store, St. Basil's Cathedral, Lenin's Mausoleum, and the eastern walls of the Kremlin, which is the true heart and historical jewel of the city.
The Moscow style of Art Nouveau is well-represented by a visit to the Ryabushinsky House (now the Gorky Museum). The cylindrical Melnikov House, the Rusakov club by the same architect, the Zuev workers' club by Golosov, and the Narkomfin collectivist house by Ginzburg are the best ex-

amples of the avant-garde period, which also includes the Tsentrosoyuz by Le Corbusier.
The various phases of Stalinist architecture, which culminated in the famous seven skyscrapers, are best illustrated along the city's main radial axes, in particular Tverskaya ulitsa, Leninsky prospekt, and Leningradsky prospekt, as well the Sadovaya ring road.
The Schusev State Museum of Architecture (MUAR) offers a rich program of temporary exhibitions as well as the extraordinary seventeenth-century wood model of the Kremlin on permanent display.
The Ostozhenka district, adjacent to the reconstructed Cathedral of Christ the Savior, contains the best concentration of works of contemporary architecture from the post-communist period.
The Pushkin Museum hosts European, Middle Eastern, and Asian art collections, in addition to the world-famous paintings from the Impressionist and Post-Impressionist periods.
The State Tretyakov Gallery displays beautiful collections of Russian fine art, with works from the 11th to early 20th centuries at the Staraya Tretyakovskaya, and the not-to-be-missed avant-garde works of the 20th century at the Novaya Tretyakovskaya.
One of Moscow's main architectural attractions is a tour of the spectacular "underground palaces" of its historic metro stations, in particular along Line One (red), Line Two (green), and the Circle Line (brown).

5. Bird's-eye views of Moscow_ Beautiful panoramic views can be enjoyed from the restaurants of the historic Ukraina and Leningradskaya hotels, as well as from the Ostankino towers and the Federation Tower.

6. Documents_ Police conducting ID checks may ask you for your passport and other documents. Some people prefer to leave the originals in their hotel and carry photocopies when they go out. Travelers who spend more than seven workdays in Russia (including Saturday, counting from the date of entry at the airport) must register their entry visa. If you are staying at a hotel, the management will take care of registration. If you are staying in a private home, you should find out how to register your visa before arriving in Russia. Do not lose the migration card that is issued to you at the port of entry, as you must submit it to immigration authorities upon departure.

7. Money exchange_ If you do not already have local currency, change a small amount of money for rubles upon arrival at the airport. Once you reach the city, you will find an endless number of exchange offices, clearly visible from the street. They are open at all hours and offer much better exchange rates.

Moscow Historical Introduction

Alessandro De Magistris* / Umberto Zanetti**

Moscow, the capital of the Russian Federation, was founded in the 11th century at the confluence of the Neglinnaya and Moskva rivers. Its layout is based on a ring-road system, with streets radiating out from the Kremlin, which was originally a fortress and the center of political and religious power. Initially built in wood, as was the entire settlement, the Kremlin was surrounded by walls in white limestone from the 13th-14th centuries, a period of great artistic and building impulse that placed Moscow amongst the ranks of such older cities as Kiev, Novgorod, and Vladimir.
The limestone walls were replaced in the 15th century by the red brick fortifications that are still visible today. The layout and urban fabric that continued to characterize the development of Moscow took form during the gradual expansion of the city during the 18th and 19th centuries. After the revolution and throughout the 20th century, Moscow, as the capital of the Soviet State, underwent important changes that confirmed its status as Russia's preeminent urban center. Its role as a model communist city is reflected in both the architecture and in the urban development projects promoted by the various general plans drawn up during the Soviet era, beginning with the historic *Genplan Rekonstruktsii* of 1935.
The early 20th century is deeply permeated by eclecticism and by the extraordinary expressions of Art Nouveau (in Russia *novyj stil'* or *modern*). The Revolution marked a radical break with the past. Increasingly ambitious urban works from the 1920s clearly reflected the range of opportunities, directions, and original developments of Soviet design culture at that time. The initial directions in which the various and opposing avant-garde trends expressed themselves are represented by such masterpieces as the Narkomfin collectivist apartment house (Ginzburg), Melnikov's cylindrical house, and the Rusakov (Melnikov), the Zuev (Golosov), and the ZiL (A. Vesnin) workers' clubs.
The openness towards experimentation of those years also applied to Le Corbusier. A leading figure of Western design culture, he built in Moscow the innovative and imposing Tsentrosoyuz Building, headquarters of the union of cooperatives.
With Stalin's rise to power and the long Stalinist era came eclectic manifestations of the "Socialist Realism" that reshaped the city from the 1930s through the 1950s. This moment in history can be read in the Metro stations, the monumental buildings, the gigantic administrative complexes and residential blocks (*kvartaly*), and, as the final expression of the Stalinist era, the skyscrapers (*Visotky*) that went up in celebration of Russia's victory in the Great Patriotic War (World War II).
The advent of Khrushev and de-Stalinization led to the rejection of monumentalism and initiated a period of industrialization of construction processes aimed at providing solutions to the dramatic and endemic housing shortage.

This resulted in the construction of immense residential districts (*rajony*) with standardized services, inspired by a productivist modernism that marked a reconciliation with the International Style of the Western countries. This functionalist approach of mass construction continued to characterize the architectural production of the final decades of Soviet Moscow.

PROSPECTS FROM THE 1990S THROUGH TODAY

With the dissolution of the USSR, a new phase of pressing and radical transformation took shape in the early 1990s, accompanied by the privatization of the economy and the revival of the real estate market. The rigid planning tools in force until the 1980s were replaced by profoundly different prescriptions, summarized by the "Moscow 2020" plan and its updated version, "Moscow 2025." The most significant episodes of post-socialist Muscovite architecture has been driven by investments in the service sector, in particular banks and office and commercial complexes, and in the construction of luxury homes. These buildings reflect a decisive renewal of the city's architectural culture, accompanied by a rebirth of the profession of architect and initially dominated, with rare exceptions, by an eclectic approach expressed through the commercial banalization of historic motifs.
More recent times, following changes in the top tiers of city government, have been characterized by a new scale of operations involving the redefinition of the relationships between the city center and its regional context. Among the issues and important urban developments being addressed, also by means of international competitions, are the Moscow City business center, which is nearing completion, the refurbishment of the vast Soviet legacy of long-abandoned industrial areas, the infill of urban voids, and the renovation of large public spaces and parklands. An essential part of the latest phase of modernization consists in the upgrading of infrastructures, in particular the Metro network and links between the city and the airport.
Another significant aspect is the increasing awareness of the importance of – and the importance of preserving – the city's heritage of avant-garde architecture, which is seriously threatened by degradation and speculation.

* Architect, Full Professor (Politecnico di Milano)
** Civil Engineer (Politecnico di Milano), founder of the architecture firm ZDA

Moscow City
Hotel Ukraina
MID
Cathedral of
Christ the Saviour
House on the
Embankment

Barrikadnaya
Novy Arbat
MUAR
Lenin Library
Pushkin Museum
Kremlin
© Denis Esakov

Zamoskvorechye

MGU
Gorky Park
Garage
Luzhniki Stadium
Novaya Tretyakovskaya
Ostozhenka
Krasny Oktyabr
Strelka
House on the Embankment
Udarnik Cinema

Strategies for visiting Moscow

A | Kremlin - Historic City Center

The Kremlin - Historic City Center itinerary rotates around the historic center of Moscow, between the Moskva River and the Bulvar ring roads. The composite character of this area bears witness to the city's layers of history and the constant transformation of its urban fabric to this day. The Kremlin, Moscow's earliest fortified village, is bound by a system of large public spaces, consisting principally of the **Red Square**, within which stands **Lenin's Mausoleum/01**, and **Manege Square/03**, whose renovation with an underground shopping mall was an emblematic redevelopment project of the 1990s. Moscow's most famous religious and civic monuments are concentrated in a limited area that has always remained the heart of the city. In addition to the Kremlin and the **Cathedral of Christ the Savior/14** are a number of cultural buildings, including the Pushkin Museum, the Muar Museum, the **Lenin Library/13,** the Bolshoi Theater, and the MKhAT. The district is crossed radially by a major traffic artery, **Tverskaya ulitsa/06**, and also encompasses such historic commercial buildings as GUM/02, TSUM/09, and Detsky Mir/10, Soviet and government buildings, including the KGB building/11 and the State Duma, and the headquarters of service-sector companies, including Northern Insurance/04 and the Central Telegraph Office/07. The center of Moscow has been an elite residential district throughout its history. Here we find Mokhovaya House/05, **Dinamo Society Building/12**, and **Bryusov residential building/08**, as well as several historic hotels: Hotel National, Hotel Moskva, and Hotel Metropol.

B| Ostozhenka - Novy Arbat - Moscow City

Numerous experimental buildings have sprung up in Ostozhenka since the early 2000s, redesigning the fabric of the neighborhood. Such structures as the **Unicredit Bank/21, Maple House/22**, **Copper House/16,** the **Butikovsky/20**, **Barkly Plaza/15** and **Ether/19** office towers, and the **Molochny/18** and **Korobeynikov/23** residential complexes have transformed the district into one of Moscow's most prestigious and attractive parts of the city. In contrast to their modern style, the nearby **Pompeii House/33** is an excellent work of refined contemporary eclecticism. The Frunze quarter, which extends north from the Frunzeskaya embankment along the Moskva River, was traditionally occupied by the Red Army and contains the Frunze Military Academy/28 and the Kauchuk Factory Club/27. Nearby are two modern building complexes, **Fusion Park/25** and Burdenko/29, along with the **Levshinsky residential complex/30**, the facades of which reinterpret the classic canons. In the early 1960s, Khrushchev demolished a picturesque neighborhood to make way for **Novy Arbat/34**, as part of his project for modernizing the city. The old ulitsa Arbat, a remnant of this historic fabric, was pedestrianized in the 1980s and has become an important tourist attraction. In the vicinity are the **Melnikov house and studio/32,** today a branch of the MUAR Museum of Architecture, and the

Narkomfin collectivist residential building/36. At the intersection with Kutuzovsky Prospekt, Novy Arbat culminates with the SEV-Comecon headquarters/38, the Russian White House/37, and the Hotel Ukraine. To the northwest, in tangent to the Third Ring, is the new business center, **Moscow City/40**, with its interesting collection of international high-rise styles.

C| Tverskaya - Belorusskaya

The historic link between Moscow and St. Petersburg, **Tverskaya Street/06**, became, under the Stalinist regime, a point of reference within the new urban landscape. The first section of the street, after it crosses the Bulvar, opens onto Pushkinskaya Square, which is overlooked by the **Izvestiya newspaper building/48** and the Rossiya Theatre/50. The **Utro Rossii printing house/49** is also close by. On either side of the Sadovoye Koltso (the Garden Ring), from east to west, are notable examples of Modernism/Art Nouveau, for instance the Ryabushinsky Mansion, Gorky Museum/42, and of avant-garde Soviet architecture, for instance the **Mostorg Department Store/45**. Interesting works of contemporary architecture include the headquarters of the Union of Architects of Russia/41, the **Granatny residential complex/43**, and the **Patriarkh residential complex/47**, which looks onto the charming Patriarch Ponds residential area. Continuing on, we reach Mayakovskaya Square and the **Mayakovskaya Metro Station/52**, which is an ideal starting point for an itinerary in discovery of the "underground palaces," the historic stations of the first Metro lines. Not far from here is the **Penguin office building/53**, and, at the far end of this section of the Koltso, the recently built **Tsvetnoy Central Market/51,** by the firm Meganom. Traveling along Tverskaya, moving outward from the city center, we find the Belorusskaya station. Numerous office complexes have sprung up around this important node, among which **Belaya Ploshchad/56**, which is not far from the **Zuyev Club/55,** one of the most famous examples of workers' clubs built towards the end of the 1920s. On Leningradsky Prospekt, just before its intersection with the Third Ring, is the **Experimental residential building/58** and, in the vicinity, the Begovaya residential complex/57, inspired by le Corbusier. In the eastern part of this itinerary are two historic structures, the Pravda/59 and the **Ex-Garage Bakhmetevsky/60**, as well as the recently built **Federal Court of Arbitration of the Region of Moscow/54**.

D| Chistye Prudy - Sretenka - Prospekt Mira

The northeast sector of Moscow, close to the Garden Ring, contains extremely interesting 20th century administrative buildings: the **Tsentrosoyuz/68,** the Gostorg/67, a masterpiece of early Constructivism, the **Narkomzem/64**, the Ministry of Transport/65, one of the seven Stalinist skyscrapers, and, adjacent, the NKPS People's Commissariat of Transportation/66. A little farther out is the Yaroslavsky railway station/62. It is a remarkable work of Art

Nouveau architecture and one of Moscow's most important transport nodes. Among the many interesting examples of adaptive reuse in this part of the city are **Art House/72**, along the Yauza River, **Winzavod/71**, the historic wine factory converted into a center for contemporary art, Gazgolder/70, which has been converted into a multipurpose center, and the new office building complex, **BO 2-M/61**. Nearby is an excellent example of late-Soviet cultural architecture, the **Taganka Theater/74**.

E| Zamoskvorechye

The area encompassing Bolotnaya Island and the Zamoskvorechye district have always been industrial in nature, and still retain many of the same features and charm. After crossing the historic Bolshoy Kamenny bridge, we encounter interesting examples of Soviet residential architecture, such as the imposing **House on the Embankment/76**. Continuing along Bersenevskaya Embankment, we arrive at the **Strelka Institute/77**, one of the most important features of the new Moscow, and Krasny Oktyabr, a former industrial area that is currently undergoing major transformation.
On the Kadashevskaya Embankment we reach the new Tretyakov Gallery, which has an extraordinary collection of avant-garde Soviet and 20th-century works. Across from the gallery is the entrance to **Gorky Park/78**, Moscow's principal recreational area during Soviet times. Today, Gorky Central Park has been fully revived as a cultural and recreational center, also hosting **Garage/79**, a center for art and culture. Other points on the itinerary include the MOGES-1 electric power plant/75, a masterpiece of Soviet industrial architecture, and the modern office complexes **Vivaldi Plaza/83** and **Ozerkovskaya/84**. Further south is the Shabolovskaya neighborhood, which contains the **Shabolovka residential complex/80**, the student dormitory complex/82, and the **Shukhov Radio Tower/81**, an extraordinary steel structure.

F | North

This itinerary encompasses a vast area characterized and organized around the presence of the principal road and rail links situated in the northern part of the city, including the Leningradsky, Butyrskaya, and Mira metro stations. Along these main routes and surrounding areas are various examples of contemporary architecture, as well as a number of masterpieces of Soviet architecture. In particular, from the 1920s, are the **Rusakov/99** and Burevestnik/98 workers' clubs. The **VDNKh/95** trade show complex and amusement park was built between the 1930s and 1950s. Interesting examples of contemporary residential architecture include, among others, the **Aerobus mega-complex/88** and the **VDNKh tower/94**. As regards the new generation of office buildings, particularly worth mentioning are **Mercedes-Benz Plaza/86**, **Metropolis/90, AG Metro/91**, **Siemens AG/87**, and **Alkon 1/89,** along Leningradsky Prospekt, and the new **Aeroflot headquarters/93** and the **Khimki Business Park/92**, adjacent to Sheremetevo Airport.

G| East

The southeast part of the city, which extends along Entuziastov Shosse and the banks of the Moskva River as far as the Danilovsky District, attests to the Soviet regime's emphasis on large-scale manufacturing in its drive to industrialize the country. The area was occupied by enormous factories and industrial sites, including GPZ-1, AZLK, Serp & Molot, and the ZiL automotive plant/104. Competitions were recently held for the renovation and adaptive reuse of the latter two factories. Workers' housing complexes and cultural centers, including the **ZiL Cultural Center/102**, were built in close proximity to the factories. The **Stanislavsky Factory/100** is an excellent example of the successful conversion of one of these former industrial sites. Two additional buildings of great interest on this itinerary are the 1930s Gosplan Parking Garage/105 by Konstantin Melnikov, and the **Dominion Office Building/101** by Zaha Hadid.

H| South

The southern periphery of Moscow, served by major transport arteries, had been set aside for high-density housing development since the 1920s. This policy was reconfirmed and intensified during the postwar period (the 1949-51 plan) and in the 1960s-1970s. The **Southern Experimental Districts/108**, including Novye Cheryomushki, Yugo-Zapadny/121, Chertanovo Severnoye/114, Nagatino/116 and Yasenevo/115, represent some of the most emblematic housing projects from the city's various periods of expansion. The **House of the New Way of Life/107**, a complex of communal apartments, was presented as a prototype for collectivist living. Particularly interesting recent structures include the **Danilovsky Fort/106** and **Nauchny Park/111** business centers, the **Avant-garde residential tower/110**, and the **Avenue 77 residential complex/113.**

I| West

The western district of Moscow is heterogeneous, with both remarkable historic buildings and a number of works of contemporary architecture. In the first category are the Stalinist **Moscow State University/118**, and the **Mosfilmovskaya Building/117**, along with the Luzhniki Olympic Complex (which includes the former Central Lenin Stadium), which also served as a venue for the 1980 Olympics. The three modern developments on this itinerary lie in the easternmost part of the district: Skolkovo Technopark, with the buildings **Hypercube/125** and **Matrex/124**, the **Moscow School of Management/123**, and, in Barvikha, the new **Luxury Village shopping center/127**, with the adjacent **Mercury Theatre/126** and **Hotel Barvikha/128**.

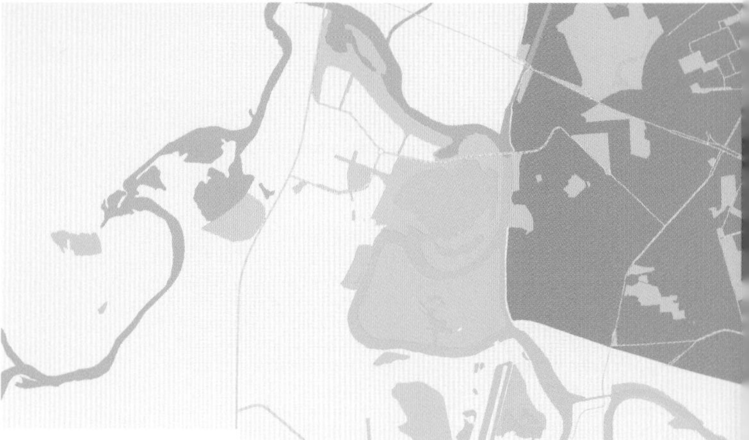

Routes

- **A.** Kremlin - Historic City Center
- **B.** Ostozhenka - Novy Arbat - Moscow City
- **C.** Tverskaya - Belorusskaya
- **D.** Chistye Prudy - Sretenka - Prospekt Mira
- **E.** Zamoskvorechye
- **F.** North
- **G.** East
- **H.** South
- **I.** West

F
C
D
A
B
E
G
I
H

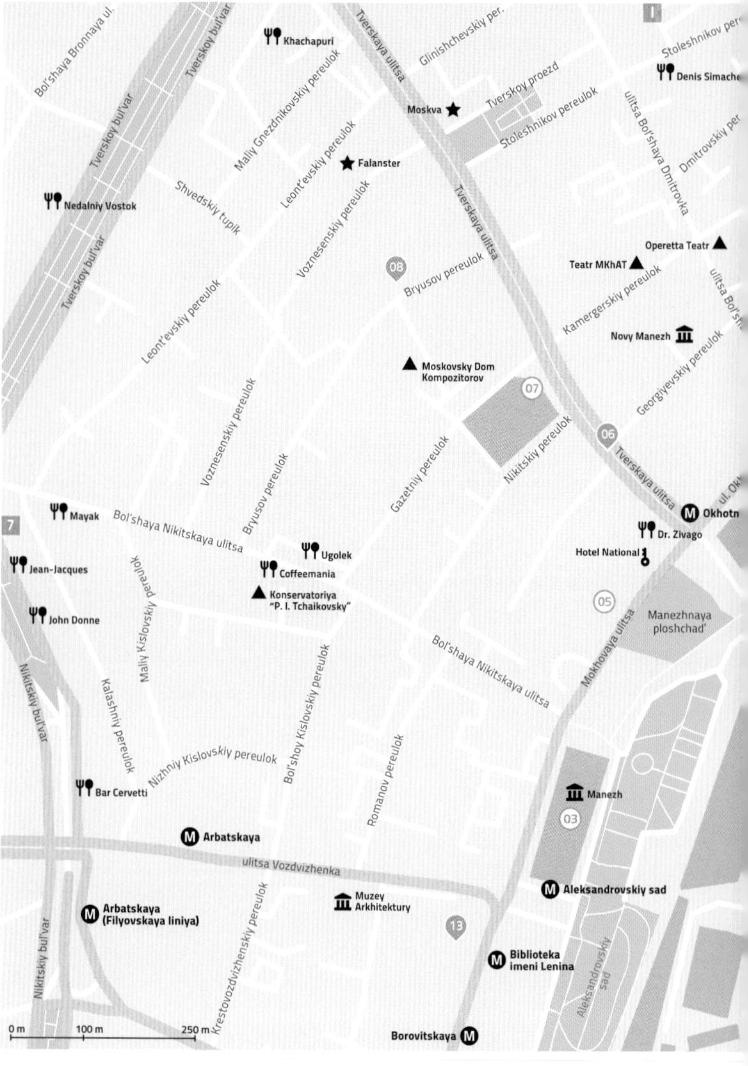

Bol'shaya Bronnaya ul.
Tverskoy bul'var
Khachapuri
Tverskaya ulitsa
Glinishchevskiy per.
Stoleshnikov per.
Denis Simache
Tverskoy proezd
Moskva
Maliy Gnezdnikovskiy pereulok
Stoleshnikov pereulok
ulitsa Bol'shaya Dmitrovka
Dmitrovskiy per.
Falanster
Leont'evskiy pereulok
Shvedskiy tupik
Nedalniy Vostok
Voznesenskiy pereulok
Operetta Teatr
Teatr MKhAT
Bryusov pereulok
Kamergerskiy pereulok
ulitsa Bol'sh
Novy Manezh
Georgiyevskiy pereulok
Moskovsky Dom Kompozitorov
Gazetniy pereulok
Nikitskiy pereulok
ul. Okh
Okhotn
Mayak
Bol'shaya Nikitskaya ulitsa
Dr. Zivago
Ugolek
Hotel National
Jean-Jacques
Coffeemania
Konservatoriya "P. I. Tchaikovsky"
Maliy Kislovskiy pereulok
John Donne
Manezhnaya ploshchad'
Mokhovaya ulitsa
Nikitskiy bul'var
Kalashniy pereulok
Bol'shoy Kislovskiy pereulok
Nizhniy Kislovskiy pereulok
Romanov pereulok
Bar Cervetti
Manezh
Arbatskaya
ulitsa Vozdvizhenka
Aleksandrovskiy sad
Muzey Arkhitektury
Arbatskaya (Filyovskaya liniya)
Krestovozdvizhenskiy pereulok
Biblioteka imeni Lenina
0 m
100 m
250 m
Borovitskaya

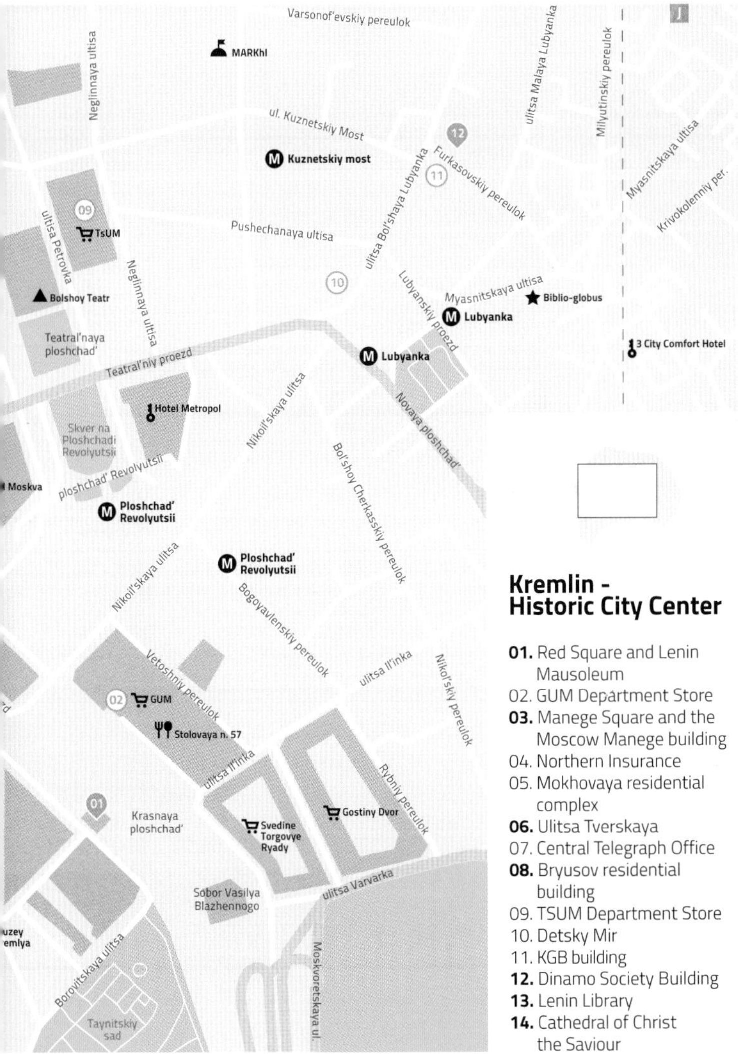

Kremlin - Historic City Center

01. Red Square and Lenin Mausoleum
02. GUM Department Store
03. Manege Square and the Moscow Manege building
04. Northern Insurance
05. Mokhovaya residential complex
06. Ulitsa Tverskaya
07. Central Telegraph Office
08. Bryusov residential building
09. TSUM Department Store
10. Detsky Mir
11. KGB building
12. Dinamo Society Building
13. Lenin Library
14. Cathedral of Christ the Saviour

01. Red Square and Lenin Mausoleum

Krasnaya ploshchad
101000 Moscow

January - December
Tue - Thu / 10 am - 1 pm
Sat / 10 am - 1 pm
Mon - Fri - Sun / closed

+7 (495) 6235527

www.lenin.ru

1 > Okhotny Ryad;
2 > Teatralnaya;
3 > Ploshchad Revolyutsii

25 > Krasnaya ploshchad;
12ц/K > Teatralnaya ploshchad;
158 > Lubyanskaya ploshchad

8 > Krasnaya ploshchad;
2/12/33 > Teatralnaya ploshchad;
63 > Lubyanskaya ploshchad

The Red Square (also known as "The Beautiful Square," as the Russian words for red and beautiful share a common root), is located in the south-west section of Kitay Gorod, one of Moscow's historic urban settlements (posads) surrounded by stone fortifications. The space was originally dominated on the west by the walls of the Kremlin, and towards the Moskva River by the Cathedral of the Intercession (St. Basil's Cathedral). Its colorful and unique character is the result of a stratification of building works that culminated during the 19th and 20th centuries with the construction of the History Museum (1874-1883) and the GUM department store (1889-1893), both masterpieces of Russian eclecticism, and of Lenin's Mausoleum (1924 -1930).
GUM was Europe's largest shopping center complex when it was built at the end of the 19th century. It has a very interesting spatial organization, with three levels of arcades covered by an enormous arched glass and steel roof by the engineer Vladimir Shukhov, one of the structural pioneers of the era.

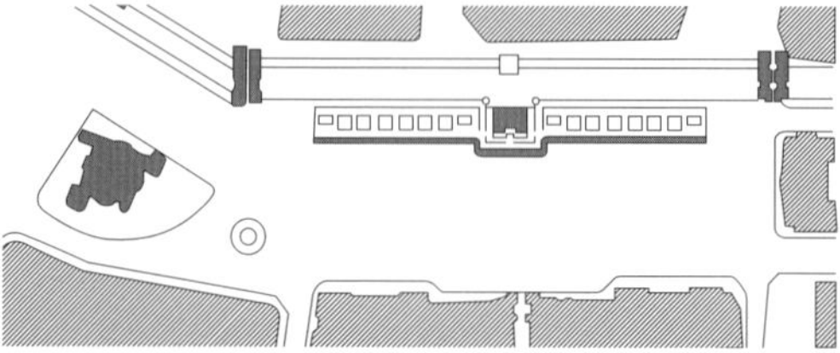

architects
A. Shchusev (mausoleum)

type
monument

construction
1924-1930

03. Manege Square and the Moscow Manege building

Manezhnaya ploshchad 1
125009 Moscow

open to public

+7 (495) 6459277
info@moscowmanege.ru
www.moscowmanege.ru

1 > Biblioteka imeni Lenina;
4 > Aleksandrovsky sad;
9 > Borovitskaya

12ц/K > Aleksandrovsky sad

1/2/12/33 > Aleksandrovsky sad

Manege Square is situated in the heart of Moscow, at the beginning of the main radial road towards St. Petersburg. For much of the 20th century it was a vast, inhospitable space devoted to motor traffic. In the 1990s it became one of the city's first and most important renovation works, heavily promoted by Moscow's mayor, Yuri Luzhkov. It was transformed into a large pedestrian zone with several levels of walkways, a multi-story underground shopping mall, and a number of architectural and sculptural works by Zurab Tsereteli. The original Manege building, a distinguishing element of the square, was built in 1817 on occasion of the fifth anniversary of the victory of the Russian army against the Napoleonic troops. In 1957, the riding academy was transferred elsewhere. In the same year, complex renovation works were begun on the facades and interiors of the Manege. On 14 March 2004, the building was damaged by a devastating fire. It was completely rebuilt, with exhibition spaces added to both the ground and basement levels, incorporating them into the original design conceived by Agustín de Betancourt and Lewis Carbonier.

© Mosproekt-2

© Mosproekt-2

architects	type	construction
A. Betancourt, L. Carbonier, G. Bove	public space	1817
Mosproekt-2, Studio 11 (reconstruction)		1993-1997

06. Tverskaya ulitsa

Tverskaya ulitsa
127006 Moscow

open to public

1 > Okhotny Ryad;
2 > Teatralnaya

12ц > Okhotny Ryad;
К > Teatralnaya ploshchad

1/12 > Okhotny Ryad;
2/33 > Teatralnaya ploshchad

One of Moscow's major urban redevelopment projects was the expansion of Tverskaya ulitsa, as provided for by Stalin's 1935 Master Plan, during which time it was known as ulitsa Gorky. The importance of this radial avenue becomes apparent when taking into account that it has linked the city centers of Moscow and St. Petersburg throughout history. Even before the Revolution, ulitsa Tverskaya was lined with businesses, hotels, and administrative offices. The Central Telegraph Office, designed by Ivan Rerberg, was erected towards the end of the 1920s.
The monumental character of the street was reinforced during the 1930s, when the roadbed was widened, some buildings were demolished, and others underwent spectacular relocation operations. The new construction was completed by a sequence of buildings inspired by the Renaissance language of Arkady Mordvinov's mixed use structures. They include the Council of Labor and Defense building, built between 1932-36 by Arkady Langman, and, directly across from it, the Hotel Moskva by Alexey Shchusev (1932-38), which has been completely rebuilt. Other important structures are the residential buildings built between the 1930s and 1940s by the architect Andrey Burov, and the Tchaikovsky concert hall at the corner of Mayakoskaya square, by Alexey Shchusev, Dmitry Chechulin, Mikhail Barkhin and others.

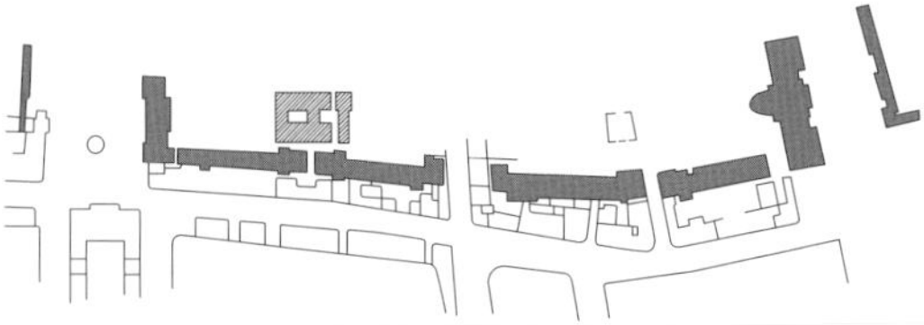

architects
A. Mordvinov, A. Burov et al.

type
infrastructural

construction
1935-1939

08. Bryusov residential building

Bryusov pereulok 19
125009 Moscow

external viewing only

1 > Okhotny Ryad;
2 > Teatralnaya;
7 > Pushkimskaya

12ц > Tverskaya ploshchad

1/12 > Tverskaya ploshchad

Designed by the studio of Alexey Bavykin, this building is located on a cross street of ulitsa Tverskaya, in the center of Moscow. Its present configuration is the result of a series of gradual transformations. Initially designed for offices, the complex was later converted to a hotel and then a residential building. Its history can be read in various details. For example, the common entrance space with its panoramic lifts hints that the building is arranged along a central corridor, common for hotels but rarer for residential buildings. The unusual layout led the architect to leave aside the classic parameters of residential construction and concentrate on the organization of the apartments themselves, resulting in innovative, high-quality solutions in terms of comfort and luminosity.

architects
A. Bavykin

type
residential

construction
2003-2006

12. Dinamo Society Building

Bolshaya Lubyanka ulitsa 12/1
101000 Moscow

external viewing only

1 > Lubyanka;
7 > Kuznetsky Most

12ц/К/158 >
Lubyanskaya ploshchad

2/12/33/63 >
Lubyanskaya
ploshchad;
9 > Vorovskogo
ploshchad

Built between 1928 and the early 1930s to a project by Ivan Fomin (1872-1936), one of the masters of Russian modernism and of the first Soviet era, this building is a superb example of "proletarian classicism."
A mixed-use complex with commercial, administrative, and residential functions assigned to the various volumes, it has become an important element of the urban context of this historic and strategic part of Moscow. The austere rhythm of the twin columns gives the building an imposing appearance. They extend the entire height of the building and appear to support an enormous entablature, emphasized by a sequence of large round windows. Across the street is the central volume of the monumental Lubyanka administrative complex, formerly the KGB headquarters (11). It was designed between the 1930s and 40s by architects Langman and Bezrukov, while the facade was designed in the postwar period by Alexey Shchusev.

architects
I. Fomin, A. Langman

type
residential, administrative

construction
1928-1932

13. Lenin Library

Vozdvizhenka ulitsa 3/5
119019 Moscow

January - December
Mon - Fri / 9 am - 8 pm
Sat / 9 am - 7 pm

+7 (495) 6955790

www.rsl.ru

1 > Biblioteka imeni Lenina;
9 > Borovitskaya;
4 > Aleksandrovsky sad

6/12ц/K > Aleksandrovsky sad

1/2/12/33/44 > Aleksandrovsky sad

The first expansion project for the Soviet Union's most important library was designed by Vladimir Shchuko and Vladimir Gelfreykh on occasion of a competition held between 1927 and 1929, a period still dominated by avant-garde ideas. The site was located at a strategic point for the reconstruction of the capital of the USSR, in the very center of Moscow, in close proximity to both the Kremlin and what was planned to be the administrative and urban heart of the city, the Palace of the Soviets. However, the library building presents a decidedly classical appearance, in conformance with the new tendencies mandated by the Stalinist regime. It consists of a complex of separate volumes with spaces for reading rooms, offices and archives. A monumental podium leading to the main entrance opens the building to multiple points of view and establishes a deliberate relationship of spatial permeability between the building and the surrounding area. The motif of the portico is elaborated by a double row of tetrahedral columns, emphasized by their cladding in polished black granite. Construction of the building was begun in the 1930s and substantially completed in 1941, though work on the interiors continued after 1945.

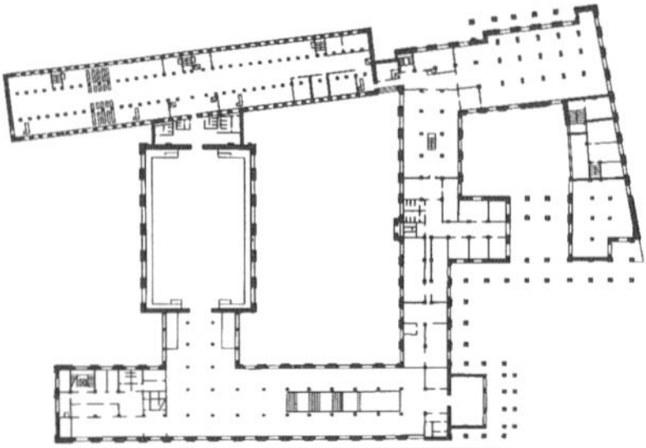

architects
V. Shchuko, V. Gelfreykh

type
cultural, educational

construction
1928-1941

14. Cathedral of Christ the Saviour

Volkhonka ulitsa 15
119019 Moscow

open to public

www.xxc.ru

1 > Kropotkinskaya

6 > Muzey Izobrazitelnykh Iskusstv;
015/05 > Kropotkinskaya

1/33/16 > Muzey Izobrazitelnykh Iskusstv;
2/15/16/31/44 > Kropotkinskaya

The cathedral we see today is substantially a faithful reconstruction — using modern building techniques — of the Neo-Byzantine church by Konstantin Thon, consecrated in 1883. It was demolished during the Stalinist era, in 1931, to permit construction of the Palace of the Soviets (designed by Boris Iofan, Vladimir Shchuko and Vladimir Gelfreykh), which was intended as a symbol of the new power. A giant statue of Lenin at the top of the Palace of the Soviets would have made it over 400 m tall, and thus the tallest building in the world at that time. It was never built, however, and during the period of de-Stalinization, the empty foundations were transformed into an open-air swimming pool that was used through the 1990s. The reconstructed cathedral was inaugurated in 1997, coinciding with the jubilee celebrations for the 850th anniversary of the founding of Moscow. The Cathedral of Christ the Savior stands on the precise spot that would have been occupied by the monumental Palace of the Soviets. Rebuilt over a stylobate that houses a lavish congress hall, its status has been restored as a symbolic landmark in the skyline of Moscow. The interior decorations and furnishings of the church feature original fragments salvaged from the destruction of the original 19th century building.

architects
K. Thon

Mosproekt-2, M. Posokhin,
A. Denisov (reconstruction)

type
place of worship

construction
1839-1883
demolition 1931
1994-1997

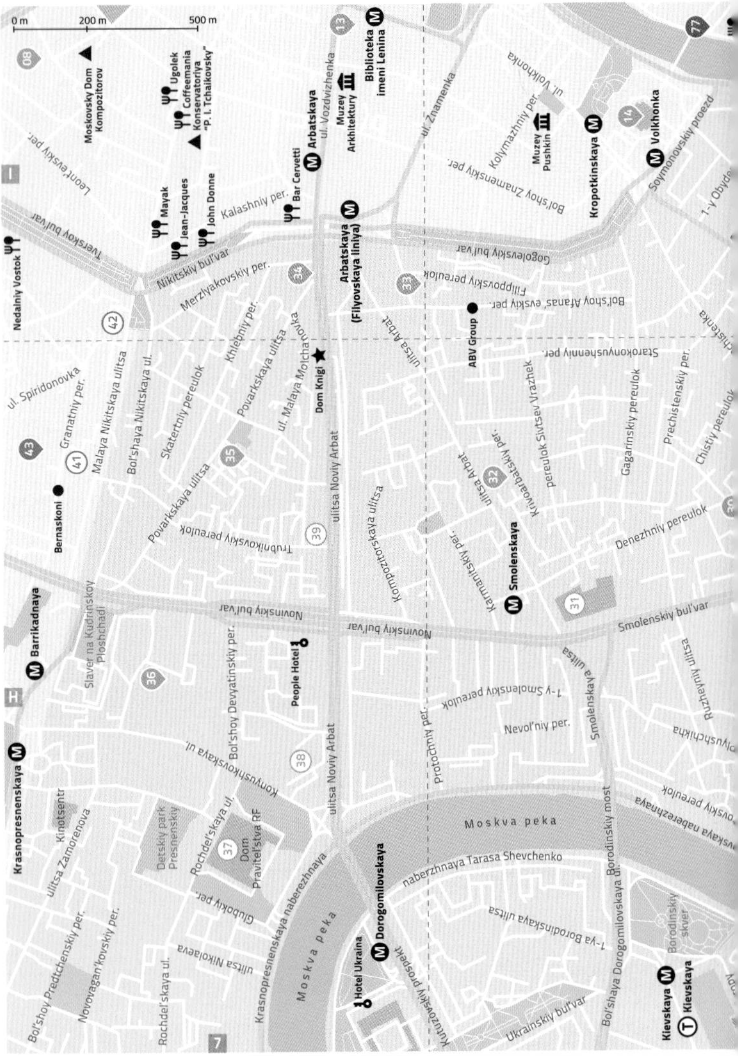
0 m
200 m
500 m
Moskovsky Dom Kompozitorov
Ugolek
Coffeemania
Konservatoriya "P. I. Tchaikovsky"
Arbatskaya
ul. Vozdvizhenka
Muzey Arkhitektury
Biblioteka imeni Lenina
Leont'evskiy per.
Mayak
Jean-Jacques
John Donne
Kalashniy per.
Bar Cervetti
Arbatskaya (Filyovskaya liniya)
ul. Znamenka
ul. Volkhonka
Kolymazhniy per.
Muzey Pushkin
Kropotkinskaya
Volkhonka
Soymonovskiy proezd
Bol'shoy Znamenskiy per.
Tverskoy bul'var
Nedalniy Vostok
Nikitskiy bul'var
Merzlyakovskiy per.
Gogolevskiy bul'var
Filippovskiy pereulok
Bol'shoy Afanas'evskiy per.
ABV Group
ulitsa Arbat
Starokonyushenniy per.
Khlebniy per.
Povarskaya ulitsa
ul. Malaya Molchanovka
Dom Knigi
ul. Spiridonovka
Granatniy per.
Malaya Nikitskaya ulitsa
Bol'shaya Nikitskaya ul.
Skatertniy pereulok
Krivoarbatskiy per.
pereulok Sivtsev Vrazhek
Gagarinskiy pereulok
Prechistenskiy per.
Chistiy pereulok
Chistenka
1-y Obydenskiy
Bernaskoni
Povarskaya ulitsa
Trubnikovskiy pereulok
ulitsa Noviy Arbat
Kompozitorskaya ulitsa
Karmanitskiy per.
Smolenskaya
Denezhniy pereulok
Barrikadnaya
Slaver na Kudrinskoy Ploshchadi
Novinskiy bul'var
Smolenskiy bul'var
People Hotel
Bol'shoy Devyatinskiy per.
Smolenskaya ulitsa
1-y Smolenskiy pereulok
Nevol'niy per.
Protochniy per.
Ruzheyniy ulitsa
Plyushchikha
Krasnopresnenskaya
Kinotsentr
Konyushkovskaya ul.
Detskiy park Presnenskiy
ulitsa Zamorenova
Rochdel'skaya ul.
Dom Pravitel'stva RF
Moskva peka
Dorogomilovskaya
naberzhnaya Tarasa Shevchenko
Borodinskiy most
Glubokiy per.
Krasnopresnenskaya naberezhnaya
1-ya Borodinskaya ulitsa
Bol'shoy Predtchenskiy per.
Novovagan'kovskiy per.
Rochdel'skaya ul.
ulitsa Nikolaeva
Hotel Ukraina
Kutuzovskiy prospekt
Ukrainskiy bul'var
Bol'shaya Dorogomilovskaya ul.
Borodinskiy skver
Kievskaya
08
13
14
77
42
34
33
43
41
35
39
32
31
36
38
37
30
I
H
7

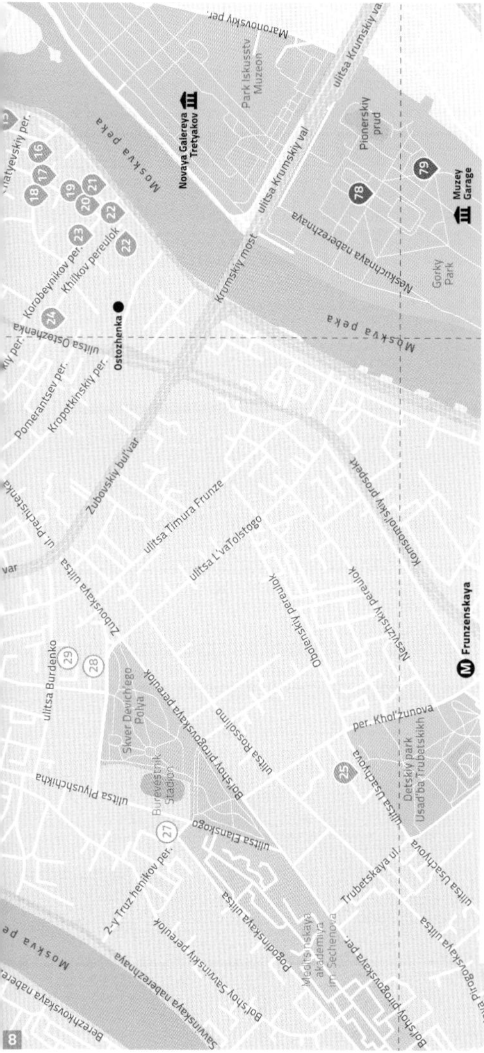

Ostozhenka - Novy Arbat - Moscow City

15. Barkly Plaza
16. Copper House
17. Butikovsky pereulok residential complex
18. Molochny residential complex
19. Ether
20. Butikovsky Offices
21. Unicredit Bank
22. Maple House
23. Korobeynikov residential complex
24. Khilkov residential complex
25. Fusion Park
26. Moscow State Academy of Choreography
27. Kauchuk Factory Club
28. Frunze Military Academy
29. Burdenko residential complex
30. Residential complex in Levshinsky
31. Ministry of Foreign Affairs
32. Melnikov House and Studio
33. Pompeii House
34. Ulitsa Novy Arbat
35. Posolky Dom residential complex
36. Narkomfin collectivist residential building
37. Russian White House
38. Sev-Comecon
39. Oktyabr Cinema
40. Moscow City

15. Barkly Plaza

Kursovoy pereulok 19
119034 Moscow

external viewing only

1 > Kropotkinskaya

31 > Zachatyevsky monastyr;
2/16/44 > Kropotkinskaya

Designed by Sergey Skuratov, the Barkly Plaza building stands out from the numerous structures that have sprung up along the quay of the recently renovated Ostozhenka district. This mixed-use complex comprises, in vertical succession, an underground parking level, a retail gallery on the ground floor, office spaces above, and luxury apartments on the topmost floors.
Divided into several volumes by an internal axis path and by the access ways along the front, the complex also reveals its composite nature through the variety of forms of the facades.
The play of volumes and the combination of materials give a sense of compactness to the lateral facades and to the side facing the Ostozhenka district and a sense of great transparency to the facade facing the river, where the apartments are arranged in a checkerboard pattern. When viewed from the other side of the river, the facades of the various volumes appear to merge into a single glazed screen, reacting instantly to the wide variety of weather and lighting conditions of Moscow.

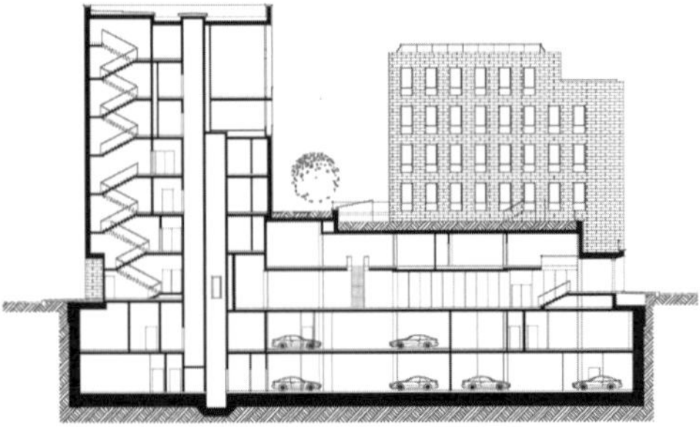

architects
Sergey Skuratov Architects

type
offices, residential

construction
2003-2009

16. Copper House

Butikovsky pereulok 3
119034 Moscow

external viewing only

1/5 > Park Kultury

2/16/44 > Kropotkinskaya; **31** > Zachatyevsky monastyr; **10/79/79к/Бк** > Park Kultury

The building takes its name from the copper cladding of the facade, making it stand out from the variegated and ever-changing landscape of the neighborhood. That the architect wanted to avoid erecting a conventional apartment building is also made evident by the unusual composition, arranged in three vertical volumes linked by a covered gallery at the ground floor. This level is occupied by two small offices. The second, third, and fourth floors of the larger volumes host two apartments each, while the fifth and sixth floors, as well as every level of the central volume, have just one apartment. The design solution creates a flowing space in the context of the variegated neighborhood adjacent to the Moskva River. The main entrance is located on Butikovsky pereulok. Visitors pass under an eight-meter high beam as they enter the complex. The lobby, in the form of a gallery, continues past two courtyards on the right, one with a swimming pool. A vestibule at the end of the gallery provides an interesting view of the path that has just been taken.

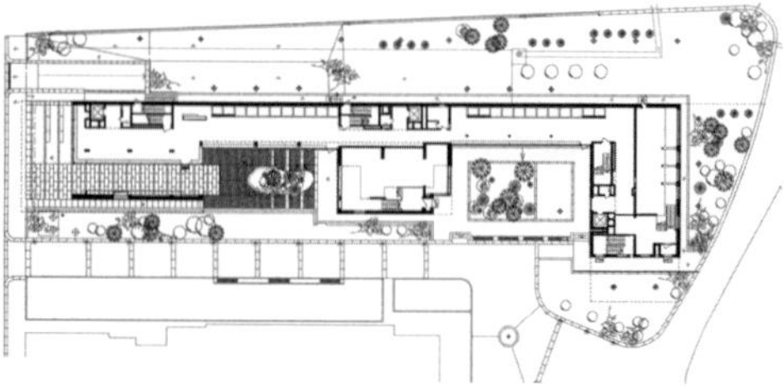

© Sergey Skuratov Architects

architects
Sergey Skuratov Architects

type
residential

construction
2002-2004

17. Butikovsky pereulok residential complex

Butikovsky pereulok 5
115184 Moscow

external viewing only

1/5 > Park Kultury

2/16/44 > Kropotkinskaya;
31 > Zachatyevsky monastyr;
10/79/79к/Бк > Park Kultury

This residential complex is located adjacent to Copper House. The project was born of a strong artistic sensibility and understanding of materials that accurately interpret the personality of the city and the specific context of Ostozhenka, one of the districts most affected by Moscow's real estate boom.
The clarity of the building layout is balanced by the variegated play of forms of the facades. The dominant motif of the facades is a material and color combination in stone, brick, wood, and metal, which gives the building a sense of both dynamism and stability. The uniformity of the materials that create this play of solids and voids across ample vertical and horizontal surfaces results in a compact, solid appearance, in contrast to the transparency and lightness of the floor-to-ceiling glazing.
The irregular rhythm of the openings underscores the diversity of functions at each level and enriches a composition which at first glance appears continuous.

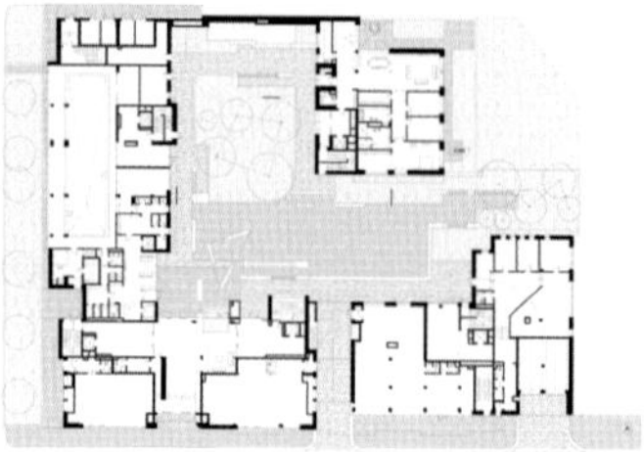

architects
Sergey Skuratov Architects

type
residential

construction
2002-2004

18. Molochny residential complex

Molochny pereulok 1
119034 Moscow

external viewing only

1/5 > Park Kultury

2/16/44 >
Kropotkinskaya;
31 > Zachatyevsky
monastyr;
10/79/79к/Бк >
Park Kultury

Built between 1998 and 2002, this building marked the affirmation of the Proekt Meganom architecture firm, inserting itself into the process of transformation of the Ostozhenka district with originality and virtuosity. By now it has become an architectural landmark. The layout of the building derives from and in turn determines the shape of the city block. The wide semicircular facade and the continuous glazed gallery form the tree-filled public space, one of the few in existence at the time of construction. Transparency at the ground floor level creates continuity between the exterior landscaping and the interior courtyard. A distinctive characteristic of the main facade is the contrast between the stone cladding, the glass parapets, and the steel structures of the secondary volumes. For this complex, erected in an area undergoing complete redevelopment, the designers and builders chose to meet the highest European standards in terms of comfort and architectural refinement.

architects
Proekt Meganom

type
residential

construction
2000-2003

19. Ether

Butikovsky pereulok 15
119034 Moscow

external viewing only

1/5 > Park Kultury

2/16/44 > Kropotkinskaya;
31 > Zachatyevsky monastyr;
10/79/79к/Бк > Park Kultury

This office building stands out for its purity of form and for the textured transparency of its louvered glass building envelope.
It stands next to the contemporary addition to the Unicredit Bank headquarters, from which it is cleanly separated by a vertical slab in reinforced concrete. This element acts as a background to a brightly illuminated full-height atrium that provides access to all of the floor levels.
The six-story building presents itself as a glass prism, broken up by the play of light of the opaline glass louvers, positioned at various angles along the facade.
This solution provides for the passage of natural light and results in lively patterns on the facade in response to changing atmospheric conditions.
The ground floor hosts the public entrance and reception spaces, as well as the cafeteria. The open-plan office spaces looking onto the atrium are flooded with natural light, which penetrates both the transparent ceiling of the atrium itself and the glass walls of the facade.
The atrium serves as a light well during the day, while after dark the interior lighting projects onto the large wall, creating interesting reflections that are visible not only from the offices but also from the exterior.

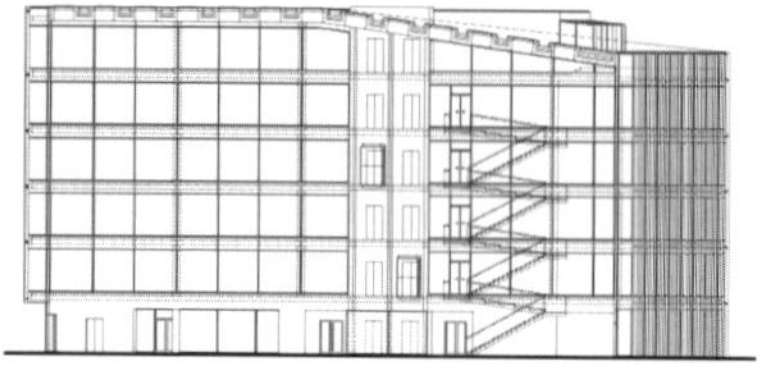

© Proekt Meganom

architects
Proekt Meganom

type
offices

construction
2008

20. Butikovsky Offices

Butikovsky pereulok 9
119034 Moscow

external viewing only

Constructed as an expansion of Unicredit Bank, this building was designed in the early 1990s by the same firm, Ostozhenka.
The new structure is completely independent, with the two buildings linked by a passageway on the second floor and by continuous parking in the two underground levels. The facade of the new expansion features a transparent, fully-glazed curtain wall protected by an articulated brise-soleil.
The horizontal blades of the brise-soleil are in terracotta, the brick color of which makes reference to the stone cladding of the original building.

1/5 > Park Kultury

2/16/44 > Kropotkinskaya;
31 > Pomerantsev pereulok;
10/79/79к/Бк > Park Kultury

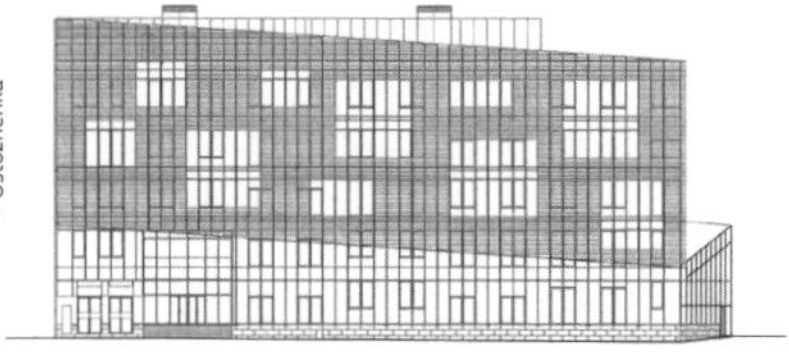

© Ostozhenka

architects
Ostozhenka

type
offices

construction
2007-2010

21. Unicredit Bank

Prechistenskaya naberezhnaya 9
119034 Moscow

external viewing only

1/5 > Park Kultury

2/16/44 > Kropotkinskaya;
31 > Pomerantsev pereulok;
10/79/79к/Бк > Park Kultury

One of the first clear signs of the capitalist transformation of Moscow was the appearance of bank branches, a building type that was absent during socialist times. Built in the early days of Russian democracy, the Meždunarodnyj Moscow Bank building was considered the most successful testimony of the new course of Muscovite architecture. The compactness and clarity of its design was in stark contrast with the noisy eclecticism of the numerous speculative projects that sprung up as the city opened itself up to market forces. The building acted as a sort of manifesto for the "critical" reconstruction of one of the few areas of the city that had escaped the planned transformations of the Soviet era. In plan, it is defined by an irregular rectangle, imposed by the historic boundaries of the site. The facade of the main volume puts the massive character of the lower portion, faced in brick and stone, in contrast with the crown, which is stepped back and surrounded by a slender framework of metal elements.

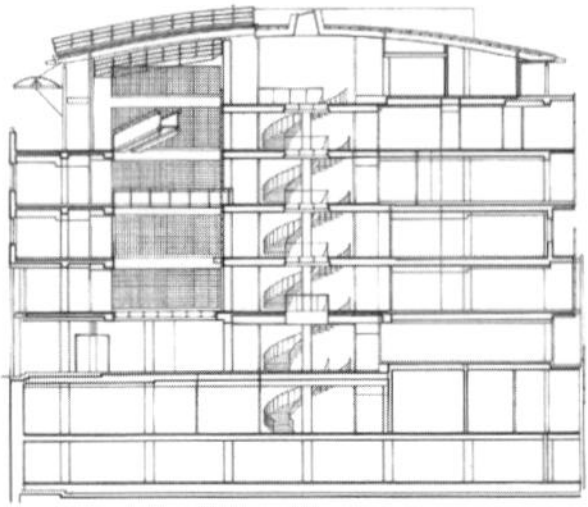

© Ostozhenka

architects
Ostozhenka

type
offices

construction
1991-1995

22. Maple House

Prechistenskaya naberezhnaya 5
119034 Moscow

external viewing only

1/5 > Park Kultury

2/16/44 > Kropotkinskaya;
31 > Zachatyevsky monastyr;
10/79/79к/Бк > Park Kultury

This mixed-use complex by the architecture firm Ostozhenka completed the reconstruction of a long, shallow lot left by the demolition of a cement factory that was to supply the construction of the Palace of the Soviets. Located along the embankment adjacent to the Unicredit Bank building, Maple House has added to the firm's repertoire of projects that have dotted and transformed the district. Articulated in three separate buildings, the largest of which starts at the corner and is attached to the Korobeynikov apartment house by the architecture firm Meganom, the complex comprises a five-story office block, a residential building on four levels, and a small hotel at the interior. The striking use of forms and materials, in particular the brick cladding and large expanses of glass, evoke the architectural characteristics of this former industrial neighborhood. The length of the building along the embankment is broken up by a zigzagged, angular facade that also multiplies the views of the windows.

© Ostozhenka

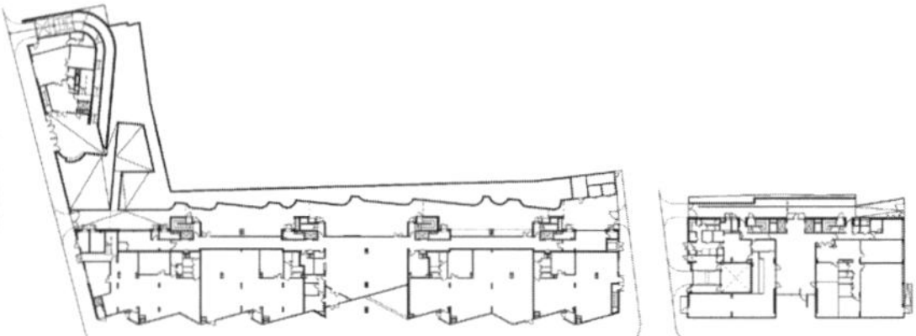

architects
Ostozhenka

type
multipurpose

construction
2015

23. Korobeynikov residential complex

Korobeynikov pereulok 1c5
119034 Moscow

external viewing only

1/5 > Park Kultury

2/16/44 > Kropotkinskaya;
31 > Pomerantsev pereulok;
10/79/79к/Бк > Park Kultury

This imposing building defines much of the entire front side of one of the lots that has re-designed Korobeynikov perulok, which today hosts a concentration of some of the best new works of architecture in Moscow. An original interpretation of the large apartment block, the building consists of two linear volumes, one opposite the other, separated by an interior courtyard and differentiated by the use of materials, in which a massive stone-clad block is perforated by two protruding glass volumes. One of the two glazed protrusions reveals the presence of a "house within the housing block." In fact, a sort of villa, distributed on four levels, is incorporated into the megastructure of this residential building, with a swimming pool below the roof. On the opposite side, the dominant theme along the street is transparency, with a series of three glass towers that permit the sun's rays to penetrate into the inner courtyard.

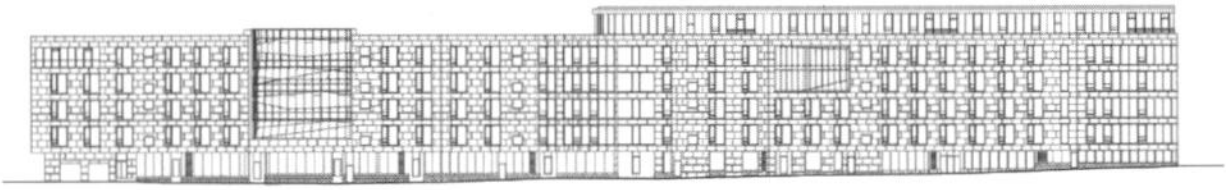

architects
Proekt Meganom

type
residential

construction
2003-2005

24. Khilkov residential complex

Khilkov pereulok 5
119034 Moscow

external viewing only

1/5 > Park Kultury

2/16/44 > Kropotkinskaya;
31 > Pomerantsev pereulok;
10/79/79к/Бк > Park Kultury

The client, Barkly Corporation, purchased this small site on the quiet side street of Khilkov pereulok, which runs from ulitsa Ostozhenka to the Moscova River. The historical roots of the neighborhood conditioned both the layout and volume of the building. Visual and solar exposure regulations dictated its low height and the unusual Z-shaped layout. This resulted in the creation of a small atrium in front of the main entrance and a quiet inner courtyard on the opposite side. The ground floor of the building is devoted to offices, while the upper floors house 27 apartments. The facade has a severe appearance and might seem too plain were it not for the relief sculptures in refractory clay at the sides of the openings, in the same pale color as that of the cladding stone. These reliefs are not random elements but fragments of the facade of the building that previously occupied the site.

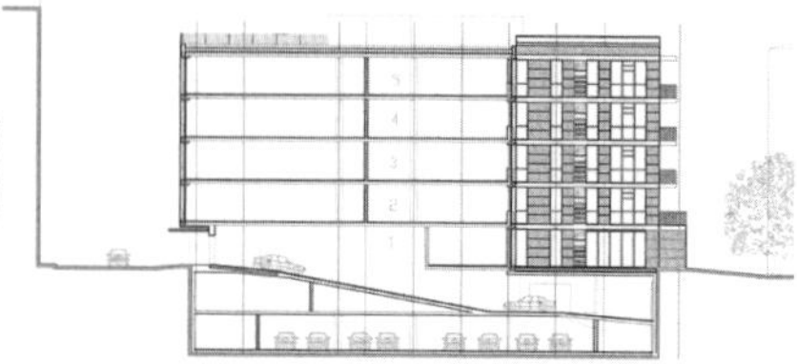

architects
ABV Group

type
residential

construction
2006-2008

25. Fusion Park

Usacheva ulitsa 2c1
119048 Moscow

external viewing only

1 > Frunzenskaya

05/015 > Ulitsa Elanskogo

15 > Ulitsa Elanskogo

The Fusion Park multifunctional complex, completed in 2008, consists of three parts: a group of apartment buildings occupying approximately 2 hectares of the 3-hectare lot, a series of office buildings located on ulitsa Usacheva, and a vintage car museum. In the original concept of the project, the three functions were meant to mingle and coexist within the same building.
The simple and severe facades of the residential buildings are punctuated by a regular succession of openings and unified by the patterns generated by the white ceramic cladding.
The urban design quality of the overall scheme is enhanced by the contrast between the residential buildings and the four adjacent office buildings, with their articulated play of solids and voids, lively zigzagged facades, and chromatic variations in the cladding materials.

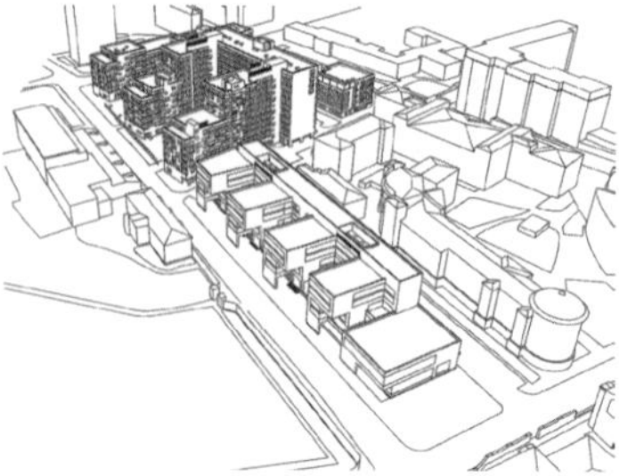

© Reserve

architects
Reserve

type
multipurpose

construction
2007-2010

30. Residential complex in Levshinsky

9/11 Bolshoy Levshinsky pereulok
119034 Moscow

external viewing only

3/4 > Smolenskaya

05/015 > Akademiya khudozhestv;
64/132 > 1-y Neopalimovskiy pereulok

15 > Akademiya khudozhestv;
Бк > Smolenskiy bulvar;
10/79/79к/132 > 1-y Neopalimovskiy pereulok

This building was designed by Ilya Utkin, who, together with Alexander Brodsky, was one of the best known of the so-called "paper architects" of the 1970s-80s. It is thus the realization of an experiment conceived according to theories that place great emphasis on the philosophy of the image.
The architect sought to create affinity with the surrounding context, the historic Arbat district, through the imaginative elaboration of the canons of classical architecture, in terms of both proportions and language.
The brickwork facade is emphasized and enriched by architectural elements in pale stone, including pilasters, columns, brackets, and trabeations, giving it a majestic appearance.
The various floors of the building take on the appearance of glazed galleries. The building is crowned by a penthouse level with a circular temple-like structure at its center. The interior courtyard was also designed in a classical style, with grottoes, shrubbery, climbing plants, and arbors. The interiors of both the shared facilities — including a swimming pool surrounded by a neo-Doric colonnade — and the apartments feature a refined classical style, combined with all the latest amenities and technological conveniences.

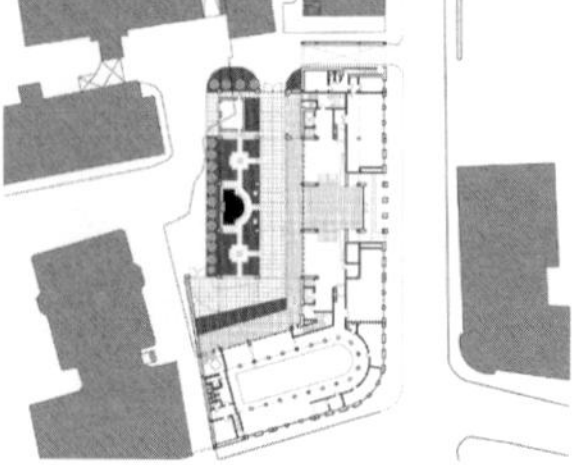

architects
Iliya Utkin

type
residential

construction
1995-2005

32. Melnikov House and Studio

Krivoarbatsky pereulok 10
119002 Moscow

open to public

+7 (499) 2640111
info@russianavantgarde.ru
www.melnikovhouse.org

3/4 > Smolenskaya

64/132 > Smolenskaya ploshchad

10/39/79/79к/Б > Smolenskaya ploshchad

Located along a narrow lane off the very central ulitsa Arbatskaya in the heart of what remains one of the most charming parts of historic Moscow, the celebrated cylindrical house and studio that Konstantin Melnikov built for himself and his family between 1927 and 1929 is one of the most original residential structures anywhere in Moscow. It is the result of a rigorous design investigation, immune to dogma of any kind, that the great architect conducted over the course of the 1920s. The structure consists of two intersecting cylindrical towers, equal in diameter but differing in height. The unusual layout of the interiors aimed to maximize the use of the circular spaces. The main facade is located in the smaller, south-facing volume, which is dominated by a large, full-height expanse of glass. It contains the dining room and kitchen at the ground floor, a double-height living room on the upper floor, and a terrace above. The second cylindrical tower, to the rear, is one floor taller and contains the bathrooms, the bedrooms, and the architect's studio, all of which illuminated by the unmistakable hexagonal windows.
Presently undergoing restoration, the building is now a decentralized branch of Moscow's Museum of Architecture and the site of organized tours.

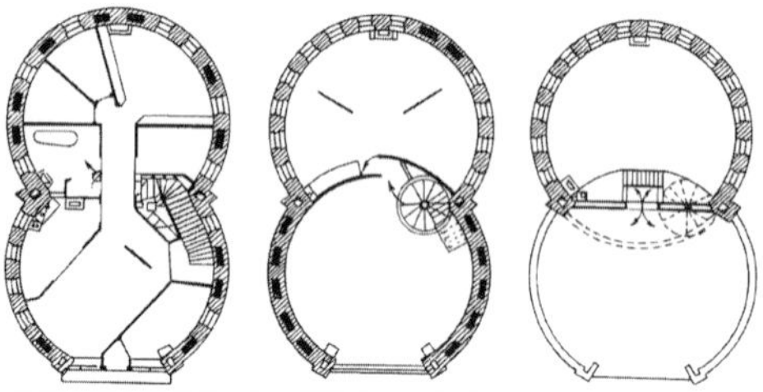

© Umberto Zanetti

architects
K. Melnikov

type
residential

construction
1927-1929

33. Pompeii House

Filippovsky pereulok 13c2
119019 Moscow

external viewing only

3/4 > Arbatskaya

6/015 > Arbatskaya ploshchad;
39 > Arbatskye Vorota

1/2/15/31/44 > Arbatskaya ploshchad;
44 > Arbatskye Vorota

One of the more interesting examples of the eclecticism that characterizes much of the architectural production of post-Soviet Moscow, this complex makes reference to a variety of sources, from Art Nouveau to the Stalin era.
The brilliant colors and rich ornamentation are clearly inspired by Pompeian frescoes. The cornice is emphasized by projecting multicolored brackets and slender columns with floral motifs, bringing to mind recurring themes in the Muscovite architecture of the early 20th century, including certain notable buildings from the 1930s by the architect Burov, located in the Tverskaya district in central Moscow.
The false historicism of the composition is justified by the location of the building, adjacent to the church of Voskreseniya Slovushchego, which dates to the 17th century. The two works of architecture appear to have been designed in the same period, as part of a single project.

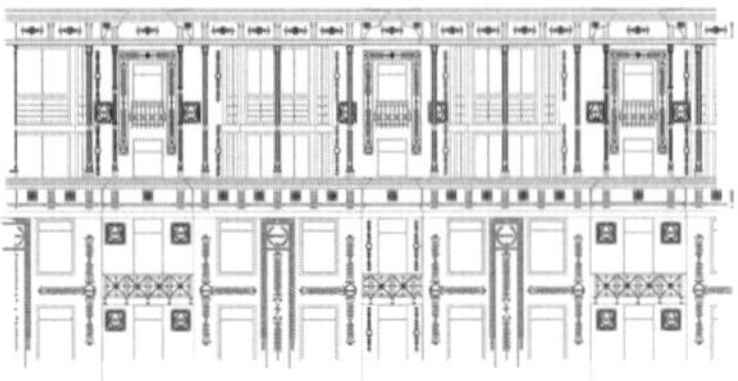

© Mikhail Belov

architects
M. Belov

type
residential

construction
2005

34. Novy Arbat ulitsa

Novy Arbat ulitsa
121069 Moscow

open to public

3/4 > Arbatskaya

6/39 > Arbatskiye Vorota

2/44 > Arbatskiye Vorota

This major artery connecting Arbat Square with the Sadovoye ring road (the Garden Ring) was built during the 1960s, partially completing the project for a road axis that had been planned prior to World War II. The aim of the operation, which resulted in the destruction of one of the districts of central Moscow that had survived the Stalinist transformations, was to create a backdrop of mega-structures along one of the major access roads to the Kremlin.
From a functional point of view, it was a re-elaboration of the mixed-use urban planning themes that characterized the image of Western cities.
The avenue runs in an east-west direction and is lined with a series of visually striking buildings designed by a collective of architects. On the south side are four imposing administrative office towers in the form of thin slabs. Each is 24 stories tall, with open-space layouts and a continuous plinth at the ground-floor level that hosts commercial activities. On the opposite, mainly residential, side of the avenue, there are five residential towers, together with the long, low volumes of the Dom Knigi bookstore, the Khleb shopping center, and the Oktyabr cinema and concert hall.
At the west end of the avenue lie the former Comecon headquarters, Hotel Ukraina, and the House of the Government of the Russian Federation (the Russian White House).

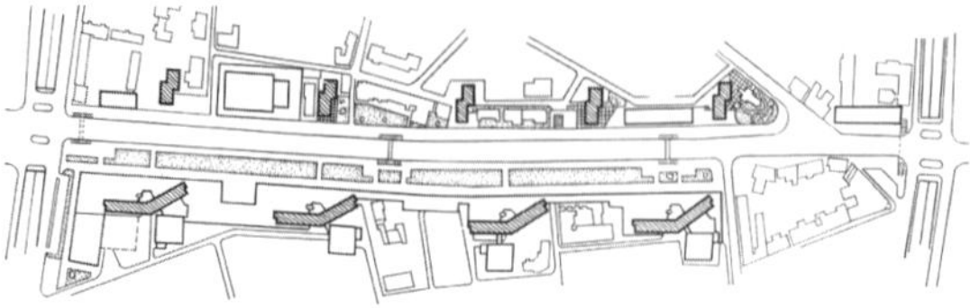

architects
M. Posokhin

type
infrastructural

construction
1962-1968

35. Posolky Dom residential complex

Borisoglebsky pereulok 13c3
121069 Moscow

external viewing only

3/4 > Arbatskaya

6/39 > Kinoteatr Oktyabr;
64 > Dom Shalyapina

10/79/Бк > Dom Shalyapina;
2/44 >Kinoteatr Oktyabr

Located along Borisoglebsky pereulok, these buildings are an obvious homage to the Melnikov cylindrical house. The urban fabric of the district underwent many changes during the last century, losing its well-defined, homogeneous character.
In the face of this situation, the location and configuration of the new construction responded to the requirements of the real estate market while also presenting the surrounding context with a new compositional rule, re-creating the dividing lines between blocks and modifying the pathways.
The residential complex is situated at a point in which the intersection of two streets forms a curve. It consists of two separate buildings, distributed over five levels and joined by a common entrance hall. The window openings, in the shape of a parallelogram inclined at 76°, reinforce the dynamism of the composition. This unusual solution gives the facades a strong identity while acting as a filter to protect the privacy of the occupants.

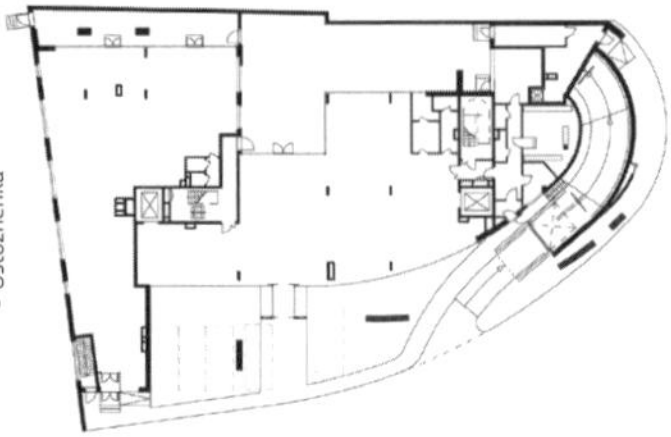

© Ostozhenka

architects
Ostozhenka

type
residential

construction
2003-2007

36. Narkomfin collectivist residential building

Novinsky Bulvar 25к1
123242 Moscow

external viewing only

5 > Krasnopresnenskaya;
7 > Barrikadnaya

6/39/64 > Kudrinskaya ploshchad

10/79/Б/Бк > Kudrinskaya ploshchad

The severe housing crisis that assailed Moscow and other Soviet cities in the second half of the 1920s, together with the influence of Western functionalism, led to a search for new residential building types, initially based on highly-compressed, flexible-use spaces for individual families, combined with an emphasis on collective functions (childcare facilities, cafeterias) and common areas. The very best example of this approach — and a masterpiece of 20th-century architecture — is the collectivist residential complex built by a cooperative of employees of the Ministry of Finance (Narkomfin) to a project by Moisei Ginzburg, Ignaty Milinis, and Sergei Prokhorov. The complex, a so-called "transitional" residential type with apartments on two floors, is articulated in a linear residential volume connected by an elevated passageway to a block of collective services. The residential volume was built on pilotis, leaving the ground level completely open. It was filled in during the 1930s to create additional housing units.
The roof was built as an accessible terrace and accommodates an independent residential unit that was originally designed to house the Minister of Finance (People's Commissariat), Nikolaj Milyutin.

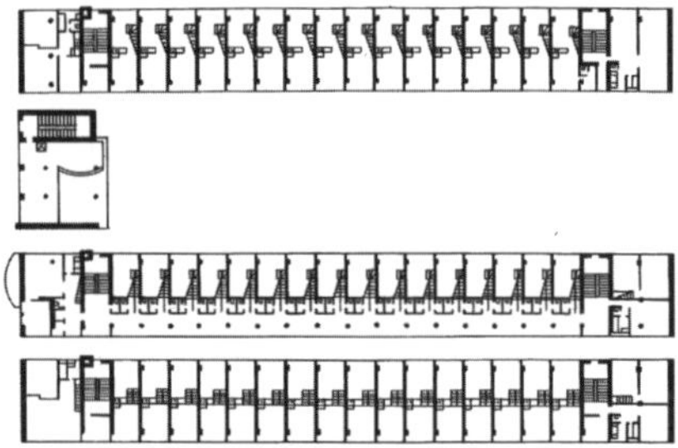

architects
M. Ginzburg, I. Milinis

type
residential

construction
1928-1930

40. Moscow City

Krasnopresnenskaya naberezhnaya 8c1
123317 Moscow

external viewing only

3 > Vystavochnaya;
3 > Mezhdunarodnaya;
8 > Delovoy tsentr

12/12a >
Vystavochnaya

The Moscow International Business Center, better known as Moscow City, is the main business and commercial district near the center of Moscow. Strategically located in terms of transport links, it lies adjacent to the Third Ring Road in the Presnensky District, in the west-central quadrant of the city.
Moscow City is destined to become Russia's major multifunctional district, combining commercial activities, offices, recreational, and entertainment facilities within a single planned development.
The planning stages of the project began in the 1990s with the elaboration of various scenarios and the subsequent involvement of a number of Russian and internationally-prominent architects. Among them was Norman Foster, whose Russia Tower was never built. At 600 meters high, it would have been the tallest building in Europe.
The main buildings that currently make up the complex are:
Bagration Bridge and the Tower 2000 office complex [0] / Expocentre [1] / Evolution Tower [2-3] / Imperia Tower [4] / Central Core [5-7] / City of Capitals [8] / Naberenzhnaya Tower [9] / Iq-quarter [10] / Eurasia [11] / Federation Towers [12] / Mercury City Tower [13] / Grand Tower [14] / Oko Towers [15] / Neva Towers [16-17] / Northern Tower [18]

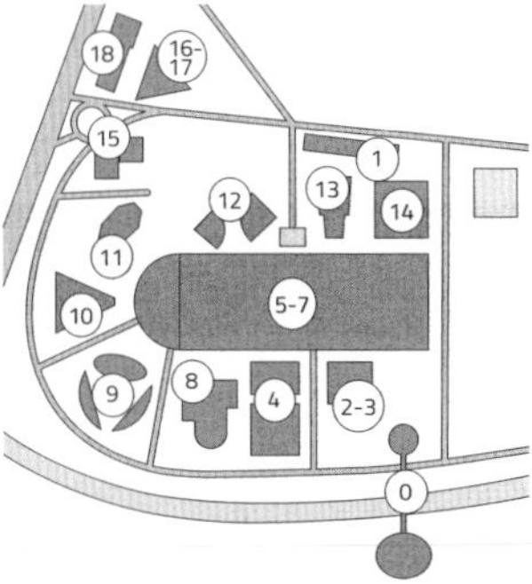

architects
various architects

type
multipurpose

construction
2005-2009

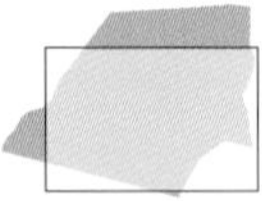

Tverskaya - Belorusskaya

41. Central House of Architects
42. Ryabushinsky Mansion, Gorky Museum
43. Granatny residential complex
44. National Center for Contemporary Art
45. Mostorg Department Store
46. Panorama residential complex and Klimashkina
47. Patriarkh residential complex
48. Izvestiya headquarters
49. Utro Rossii printing house
50. Rossiya Theatre
51. Tsvetnoy Central Market
52. Mayakovskaya metro station
53. Penguin
54. Federal Court of Arbitration of the Region of Moscow
55. Zuyev Workers' Club
56. Belaya Ploshchad
57. Begovaya residential complex
58. Experimental residential complexes
59. Pravda publishing house
60. Ex-Garage Bakhmetevsky

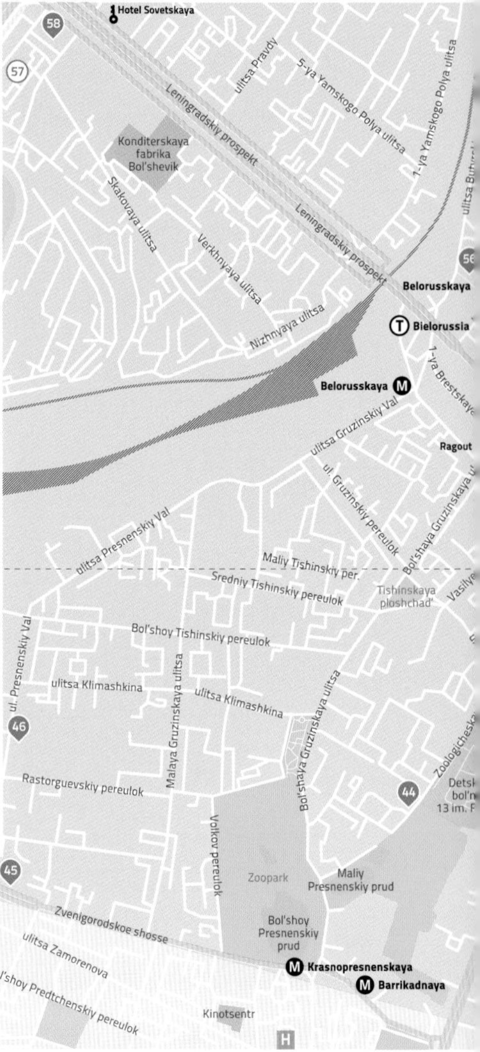

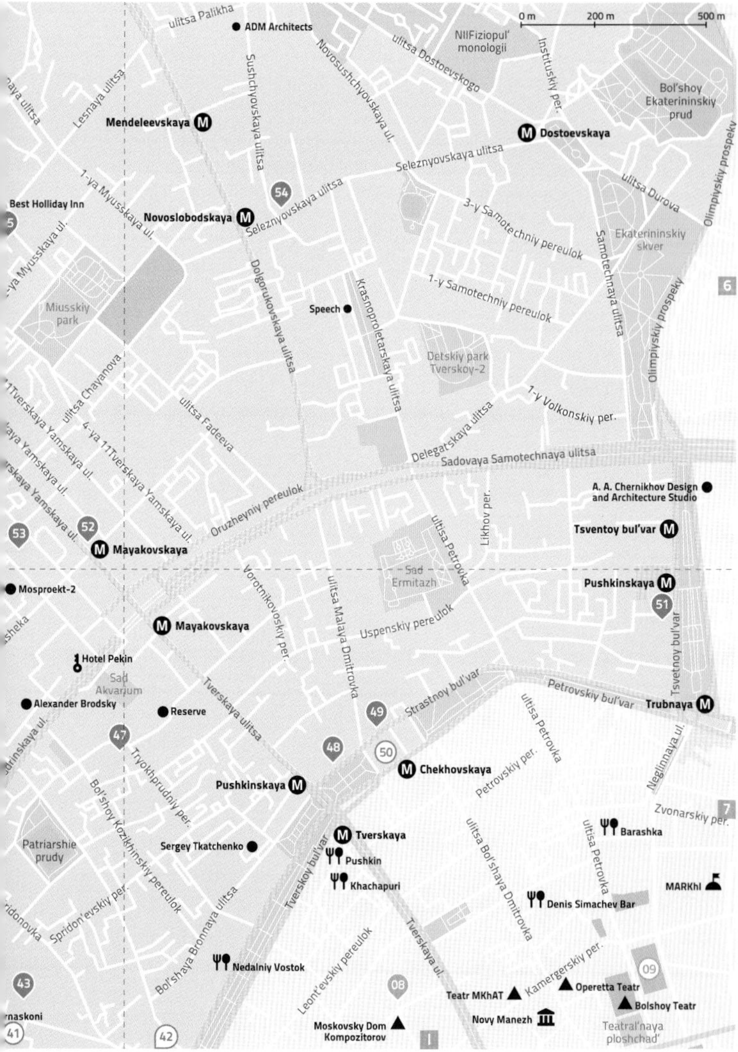
0 m
200 m
500 m
ulitsa Palikha
ADM Architects
Novosushchyovskaya ul.
ulitsa Dostoevskogo
NIIFiziopul' monologii
Institutskiy per.
Bol'shoy Ekaterininskiy prud
Lesnaya ulitsa
Sushchyovskaya ulitsa
Mendeleevskaya
Dostoevskaya
Olimpiyskiy prospekt
Seleznyovskaya ulitsa
Ulitsa Durova
1-ya Myusskaya ul.
Best Holliday Inn
Novoslobodskaya
3-y Samotechniy pereulok
Samotechnaya ulitsa
Ekaterininskiy skver
Miusskiy park
Dolgorukovskaya ulitsa
Krasnoproletarskaya ulitsa
Speech
1-y Samotechniy pereulok
6
Olimpiyskiy prospekt
Detskiy park Tverskoy-2
ulitsa Chayanova
ulitsa Fadeeva
4-ya 11Tverskaya Yamskaya ul.
Delegatskaya ulitsa
1-y Volkonskiy per.
Sadovaya Samotechnaya ulitsa
Oruzheyniy pereulok
A. A. Chernikhov Design and Architecture Studio
Likhov per.
ulitsa Petrovka
Tsventoy bul'var
53
52
Mayakovskaya
Sad Ermitazh
Pushkinskaya
51
Mosproekt-2
Vorotnikovskiy per.
ulitsa Malaya Dmitrovka
Uspenskiy pereulok
Tsvetnoy bul'var
Mayakovskaya
Hotel Pekin
Sad Akvarium
Alexander Brodsky
Reserve
Tverskaya ulitsa
Strastnoy bul'var
Petrovskiy bul'var
Trubnaya
49
ulitsa Petrovka
47
48
50
Tryokhprudniy per.
Chekhovskaya
Petrovskiy per.
Neglinnaya ul.
Pushkinskaya
Bol'shoy Kozikhinskiy pereulok
Zvonarskiy per.
7
Tverskaya
Barashka
Patriarshie prudy
Sergey Tkatchenko
Pushkin
ulitsa Bol'shaya Dmitrovka
ulitsa Petrovka
Khachapuri
MARKhI
Tverskoy bul'var
Denis Simachev Bar
Spridon'evskiy per.
Bol'shaya Bronnaya ulitsa
Leont'evskiy pereulok
Tverskaya ul.
Kamergerskiy per.
09
Nedalniy Vostok
43
08
Teatr MKhAT
Operetta Teatr
Bolshoy Teatr
41
42
Moskovsky Dom Kompozitorov
Novy Manezh
Teatral'naya ploshchad'

43. Granatny residential complex

Granatny pereulok 6
123001 Moscow

external viewing only

7 > Barrikadnaya

64 > Muzey
A. Chekhova

10/79/Бк > Muzey
A. Chekhova

The simple volumes of this residential complex are articulated with an emphasis on right angles and rhythmic vertical openings. The elevations are stylistically blended and enriched by means of ornately carved natural stone cladding. This recurring motif in the work of the firm SPEECH, by the architects Tchoban and Kuznetsov, can also be found in the noteworthy Museum for Architectural Drawing, built by the same firm in Berlin in 2009. The complex consists of three structures of different heights, linked by glass passageways and by a shared space at the basement level. The L-shape of the complex forms an interior courtyard that provides protection against street noise and recalls the traditional Muscovite residential building type, in this way relating to the context along Granatny pereulok.

© SPEECH

© Aleksey Naroditsky

architects
SPEECH

type
residential

construction
2004-2010

44. National Center for Contemporary Art

Zoologicheskaya ulitsa 11c2
123242 Moscow

open to public

+7 (499) 2540674
pr@ncca.ru
www.ncca.ru

7 > Barrykadnaya;
5 > Krasnopresnenskaya

116/116k >
Zoologicheskaya ulitsa

35 > Zoologicheskaya
ulitsa

This industrial building for set design and theater materials was converted by Mikhail Khazanov into a carefully designed exhibition and museum building devoted to the contemporary arts.
The original project, which was never built, provided for the construction of a courageous cylindrical tower, with projecting volumes that would have further emphasized the reference to constructivism.
The final version of the project preserved the original building envelope in brick, with the facades articulated by the stark red cladding of the pilaster strips and base. The industrial character of the building is emphasized by the new exterior skeleton in metal, which permitted a reorganization of the spaces and the insertion of new distribution systems.

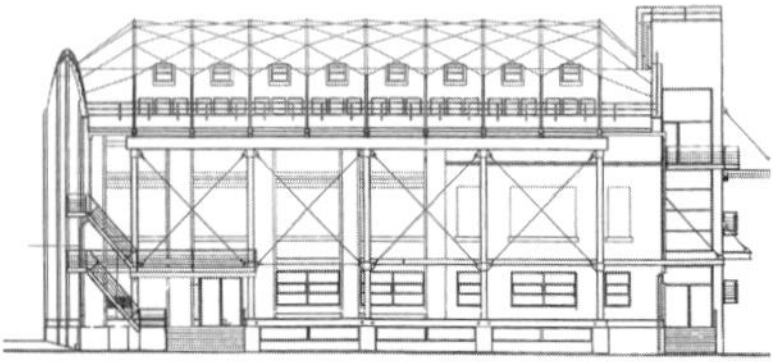

© NCCA

© NCCA

architects
M. Khazanov

type
cultural

construction
2004

45. Mostorg Department Store

Krasnaya Presnya ulitsa 48/2c2
123022 Moscow

open to public

5 > Krasnopresnenskaya;
7 > Ulitsa 1905 goda

6/39/64/69/850 >
Ulitsa 1905 goda

35/35к/79/95 >
Ulitsa 1905 goda

Completed between 1927 and 1928, the Mostorg department store was one of the first projects built in Moscow during the post-revolutionary period by the Vesnin brothers, leading exponents of the avant-garde architectural association OSA (Obedinienie Sovremennich Architektorov – Union of Contemporary Architects). It was conceived as a model building, a sort of manifesto of the constructivist "method," and even today it imposes itself in the surrounding context with the strength and clarity of a theoretical statement. The trapezoidal plan and the rear position of the stairway help make the most of the available surface area. The severe and sharply expressive facade has been partially modified but remains dominated by a large glazed surface, rounded at each side and slightly protruding with respect to the corners of the building. The building still functions as a department store today.

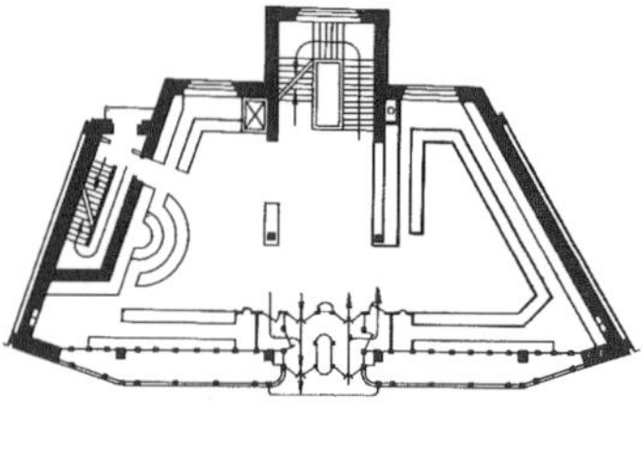

© Denis Romodin

architects
L. Vesnin, V. Vesnin, A. Vesnin

type
commercial

construction
1927-1929

46. Panorama residential complex and Klimashkina

Klimashkina ulitsa 19
123557 Moscow

external viewing only

7 > Ulitsa 1905 goda

12/12a > Ulitsa Klimashkina

18/54 > Ulitsa Klimashkina

The Panorama residential complex, by the firm Ostozhenka, is sited between the Church of the Immaculate Conception and a second complex on ulitsa Klimashkina by the same architects. The latter consists of two 15-story tower blocks linked by a pedestrian bridge at the top, in a similar compositional theme but different formal register. The raison d'etre of its solution is the axis in line with the portal of church. Though smaller, the Panorama residential complex is also articulated in two volumes separated by a narrow space, this time sinuous in form, intercepting the axis of the church. The effect is a double enfilade that affords a glimpse of the religious structure beyond the walls of the new structures. Unified by one large basement level, the two towers of the Panorama are clad with curtain walls in various tones of blue reflecting glass. Their appearance changes constantly throughout the day in reaction to changing light conditions, sometimes disappearing completely into the background of the sky.

© Ostozhenka

architects
Ostozhenka

type
residential

construction
2005

47. Patriarkh residential complex

Malaya Bronnaya ulitsa 15/44
123104 Moscow

external viewing only

2 > Mayakovskaya;
7 > Barrikadnaya;
5 > Krasnopresnenskaya

64 > Triumfalnaya ploshchad

10/79/Бк > Triumfalnaya ploshchad

This eclectic apartment building features striking and disconcertingly unusual forms that can be read as a layering of ironic citations. References to the monumental architecture of the Soviet era lead up to the crowning structure on the roof, inspired by Vladimir Tatlin's Monument to the Third International.

The building is located in one of the most picturesque and prestigious areas of central Moscow, characterized by a variegated curtain of buildings looking onto the park and pond of Patriarshiye Ponds, famous as one of the main settings of Mikhail Bulgakov's novel *The Master and Margarita.*

Nearby, on ulitsa Malaya Bronnaya, is the Gosstrakh (Soviet State Insurance) residential building, designed by the constructivist architect Moisei Ginzburg in the mid-1920s.

architects
S. Tkatchenko

type
residential

construction
2003

48. Izvestiya headquarters

Pushkinskaya ploshchad 5
127006 Moscow

external viewing only

2 > Tverskaya;
7 > Pushkinskaya;
9 > Chekhovskaya

015 > Pushkinskaya ploshchad;
12ц > Muzey Sovremennoy Istorii

1/12 > Muzey Sovremennoy Istorii;
15/31 > Pushkinskaya ploshchad;
3 > Chekhovskaya

The headquarters of the Soviet newspaper was one of the first constructivist buildings ever to be erected.
Designed in 1925, it was completed in 1927. The articulation of the volumes, concealed by the compact facade, was determined by the functional requirements of both the printing presses and the editorial staff. The facade is given a sculptural appearance by a striking combination of elements: the asymmetrical arrangement of the balconies, the vertical ribbon window running the height of the building, the contrast between the blind surface along the top of the building and the circular windows, and the grills of the window frames, enclosed between columns. The built version is quite different from the initial project, which, taking into account the belfry of the nearby monastery, had been designed along the lines of a tower building, not unlike Walter Gropius's entry for the 1922 Chicago Tribune competition. Once construction had begun, new laws restricting building heights determined the new configuration. It was integrated in the 1970s with a new, modernist building.

architects
G. Barkhin, M. Barkhin

type
offices

construction
1925-1927

49. Utro Rossii printing house

Bolshoy Putinkovsky pereulok 5
127006 Moscow

external viewing only

2 > Tverskaya;
7 > Pushkinskaya;
9 > Chekhovskaya

015 > Chekhovskaya

3 > Pushkinskaya ploshchad;
15/31 > Chekhovskaya

Designed by Fyodor Shekhtel and a masterpiece of Moscow's late Modern (Russian Art Nouveau) period, the printing house of the Utro Rossii newspaper has been converted into a cultural center. The historic features of the original industrial building have been restored, while a prismatic glazed volume has been added that houses modern vertical circulation systems. There is a cafeteria on the ground floor, spaces for associations and community use on the second floor, and large, multi-purpose open spaces and a refreshment area on the third floor. At the ground floor of the historic portion of the complex is a shop that sells vintage articles, while offices are located above. The inscription that originally crowned the main facade of the building was removed during the Soviet era to make room for two large openings. It was replaced by the restoration architects according to indications found in the archival documents.

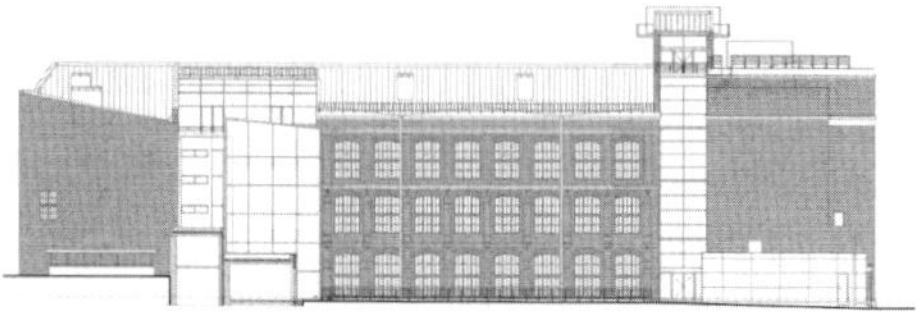

architects	type	construction
F. Shekhtel Proekt Meganom	cultural center	1907 2000

51. Tsvetnoy Central Market

Tsvetnoy Bulvar 15
127051 Moscow

January - December
Mon - Sat / 10 am - 10 pm
Sun / 11 am - 10 pm

+7 (495) 7377773

www.tsvetnoy.com

9 > Tsvetnoy Bulvar; **10** > Trubnaya

24/38 > Tsvetnoy Bulvar

13 > Tsvetnoy Bulvar

The Tsvetnoy Central Market overlooks one of the main arteries of the metropolis, near the recently built metro station of the same name. It is one of the more interesting examples of the new commercial structures that have contributed to the transformation of the urban fabric over the last 15 years, sometimes becoming landmarks in themselves. The old market was demolished and substituted with this new mixed-use building. Shops, a market, and restaurants are housed in a single, large volume, with part of the roof used as a dining terrace.
The building was conceived from the very first study models as a compact, prismatic framework, clad in stone and enclosed by large expanses of glass between the structural elements.
In the daytime this articulated solution takes on the appearance of a gigantic gemstone, while at night, the transparency of the building, enhanced by the interior lighting, makes it look more like a huge magic lantern.

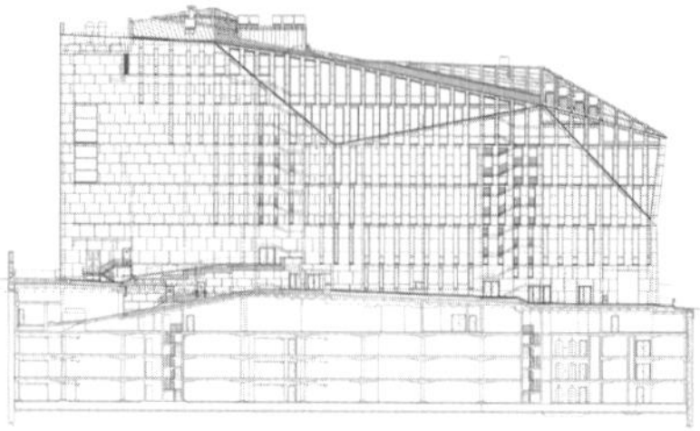

architects
Proekt Meganom

type
commercial

construction
2011

52. Mayakovskaya metro station

Tverskaya ulitsa
125047 Moscow

open to public

www.mosmetro.ru

2 > Mayakovskaya

12ц > Triumfalnaya ploshchad

1/12/3/3к/47 > Triumfalnaya ploshchad

Designed by the young architect A. Dushkin and the engineer R. Seynfan, the Mayakovskaya station, situated deep underground, is one of the most beautiful of the entire Moscow Metro. Considered a 20th century masterpiece of infrastructure architecture, it was made possible by technological improvements in the second half of the 1930s. The introduction of steel pillars in support of the vaults permitted greater design flexibility, resulting in lighter, more spacious underground environments and a greater willingness on the part of authorities to accept innovative decorative solutions. Beyond the splendid design solutions that brilliantly resolve the relationship between engineering and architecture, the station is noteworthy for its splendid ceiling mosaics, in which Alexander Deyneka (1899-1969), a prominent exponent of pictorial realism, narrated an "ideal" day in the Soviet Union.
The Moscow Metro, in particular the stations from the Stalinist period, should not be missed by anyone visiting the city. Among the many stations worth a visit are the Krasnaya Vorota, Teatralnaya, Ploshad Revolyutsi, Kropotkinskaya and Komsomolskaya stations from the 1930s, the Elektrozavodskaya station from the 1940s, and the Komsomolskaya Koltsevaya (circle line) from the early 1950s.

© Laura Andreini

architects
A. N. Dushkin

type
infrastructure

construction
1935

53. Penguin

1-ya Bretskaya ulitsa 29
125047 Moscow

external viewing only

2 > Mayakovskaya

12ц > Ulitsa Gasheka

1/12 > Ulitsa Gasheka

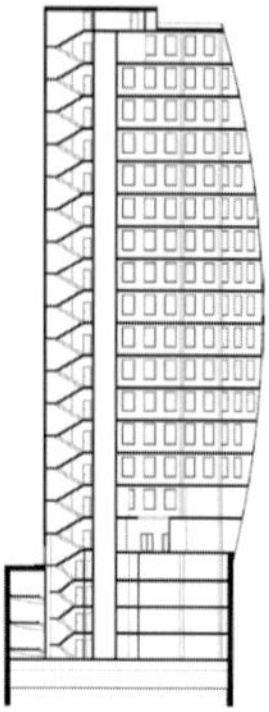

© Ostozhenka

This building by Alexander Skokan and Ostozhenka Architects aimed to enhance ulitsa Bretskaya, a street characterized by the presence of the typical bureaucratic buildings of the late-phase Soviet era. Starting from a conventional solution consisting of an office block in line with the wall of adjoining buildings along the street, the architects arrived at a surprising and disorienting solution characterized by a main facade with an unabashedly convex and projecting form that ironically interrupts the continuity of the street fronts.

This strong urban statement makes up for the ordinariness of the architectural solutions of the facade, which are solved using standard, continuous curtain wall elements. The personality of the neighborhood has been completely transfigured by this new presence, giving new significance to a street which had remained secondary and marginal, despite its vicinity to the very central Tverskaya district.

architects
Ostozhenka

type
offices

construction
2004

54. Federal Court of Arbitration of the Region of Moscow

Seleznevskaya ulitsa 9
127473 Moscow

external viewing only

7/19/19k >
Novoslobodskaya

5 > Novoslobodskaya

15/69 >
Novoslobodskaya

The Federal Court of Arbitration complex is rendered transparent and luminous by ample expanses of glass. The arrangement of the volumes around an inviting lobby, which functions as the visitors' entrance, together with the constructivist imprint of the overall composition, create a sense of hospitality and dynamism.

The complex is divided into two volumes: a seven-story office building and a three-story public building. The latter is open to visitors, who, upon entering through the reception area in the lobby, can access a variety of amenities, including shops, a dining area, and a multimedia center. The public building also houses a press office for information provided by the Court of Justice personnel. Both a spiral staircase and a lift lead up from the lobby to the second and third floor, where the court rooms are preceded by a double-height foyer.

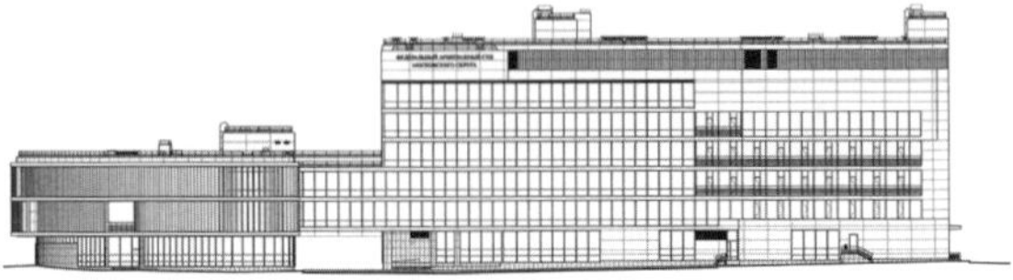

© Reserve

architects	**type**	**construction**
Reserve	offices	2004-2007

55. Zuyev Workers' Club

Lesnaya ulitsa 18
125047 Moscow

external viewing only

9 > Belorusskaya

2/5 > Belorusskaya

0/12/12a >
Belorusskaya

18/78 > Belorusskaya

In a union document from 1927, this workers' club was defined as a "laboratory" where its members could go for "knowledge, cultural entertainment, and relaxation." A series of legislative and economic measures encouraged builders to erect this type of social facility, which were commissioned mainly by the professional unions, important players during the NEP (New Economic Policy). The Zuyev Workers' Club, designed by Ilya Golosov, is considered one of the emblematic example of the rich architectural production of the period. The building hosts a large hall for meetings and performances, with seating for 850, a smaller hall, and a series of auxiliary rooms. The highly expressive juxtaposition of the volumes reveals the articulation of the interior spaces. The focal point of the composition is the glass cylinder at the corner, which houses the staircase. A recurrent theme in Golosov's work, this giant column is crowned by the slim concrete slab that forms its roof and is intersected by the rectangular volume of the lobby at the third floor.

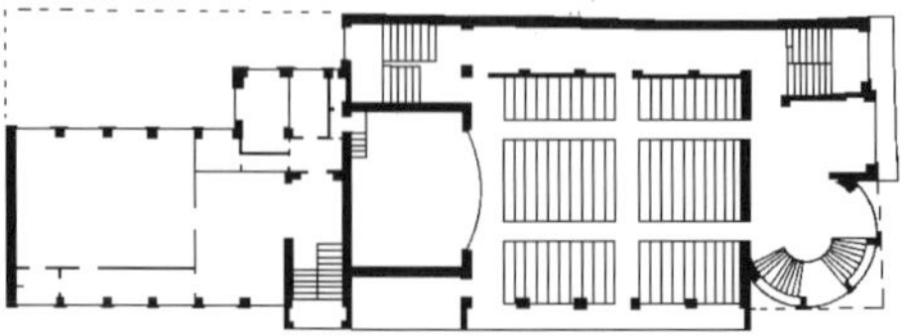

architects
I. Golosov

type
cultural

construction
1927-1929

56. Belaya Ploshchad

Butyrsky Val ulitsa 8/3
127055 Moscow

external viewing only

2/5 > Belorusskaya

Moskva Belorusskaya

1/12 > Belorussky vokzal
12/12a > Belorusskaya

12ц > Belorussky vokzal
18 > Belorusskaya

This office complex is located in a context that was already highly urbanized, near the crowded and strategically located Belorusskaya Metro station, which provides a direct link to the Sheremetyevo Airport.
Built without modifications to the existing road network, the project caused a change of scale with respect to the existing urban fabric. The tall towers of the complex occupy all of the available area between the interstitial spaces and loom over the focal point of the neighborhood, the small church of Tverskaya Staroobryadcheskaya.
The project is unified by the carefully planned urban layout, despite its fragmentation into multiple volumes and variation in facade treatment.

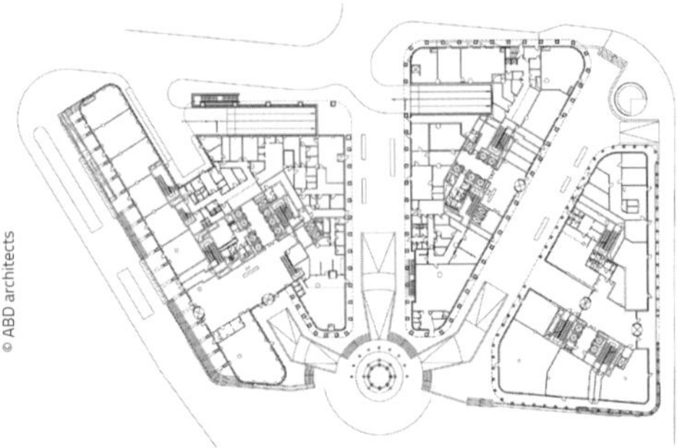

architects	type	construction
ABD architects	offices	2006-2009

58. Experimental residential complexes

Leningradsky prospekt 27
125284 Moscow

external viewing only

2 > Dinamo;
5 > Belorusskaya

12ц/27/84 > Hotel Sovetskaya

1/12/20/70/82 > Hotel Sovetskaya

Two of the most interesting experimental residential complexes from two different periods of the Soviet regime are located on Leningradsky prospekt.
The corner building shows the first example of the use of self-supporting prefabricated cladding panels. They are the result of construction science research aimed at reconciling aesthetics, as represented by the decorative plant motif on the panels, with the need to rationalize and industrialize manufacturing and construction sites. Interrupted by the war, this area of experimentation was revived between the 1940s and 1950s, but it was soon geared only to satisfying the dramatic need for housing in the rapidly developing outskirts of Moscow and other Soviet cities, with little attention to aesthetics.
Forty years later, in 1978, a 16-floor megastructure in reinforced concrete was erected in the immediate vicinity. It was clearly inspired by Le Corbusier's Unité d'Habitation, but also by similar structures in South America, which the Soviet architects watched with great interest. As with all experimental housing projects, the building prefigured and investigated possible innovative solutions, which were often made available first to the elite classes and then repeated on a large scale in cities throughout the Soviet Union.

© Denis Esakov

architects	type	construction
A. Burov, B. Blochin, A. Meerson	residential	1939-1941
E. Podolskaya		1978

60. Ex-Garage Bakhmetevsky

ulitsa Obraztsova 19A
127055 Moscow

January - December
Mon - Thu / 11 am - 9 pm
Fri - Sun / 11 am - 10 pm

+7 (495) 6450522
welcome@garageccc.com
garageccc.com

19/19k > Ulitsa Obraztsova

10 > Maryina roshcha

0 > IIT;
0 > Ulitsa Obraztsova

The brick masonry building for the Leyland bus garage on ulitsa Bakhmetevskaya was the first large commission entrusted to Konstantin Melnikov after he returned from the Paris Expo of 1925. Today it is the home of the Jewish Museum and Tolerance Center. Its trapezoidal plan was conceived by the architect to rationalize the entrance, parking, and exit of the buses. A double variation on the theme of the portal acted as a "celebratory" motif, with the sequence of numbered accesses on the main facade underscored by differentiated materials and colors. The secondary facade features circular windows that are set back into slightly projecting brick volumes, which are emphasized by full-height vertical ribbon windows. The metal roof trusses were designed by the great engineer Vladimir Shukhov.
A second bus garage by Melnikov was built in 1926-29, with an innovative semicircular plan. He returned to this building type in the 1930s with the design of car garages, in collaboration with V. Kurochkin, for Gosplan (the State Planning Commission) and for Inturist (the National Tourist Board). Their "expressionistic" forms became emblematic of the new style of architecture.

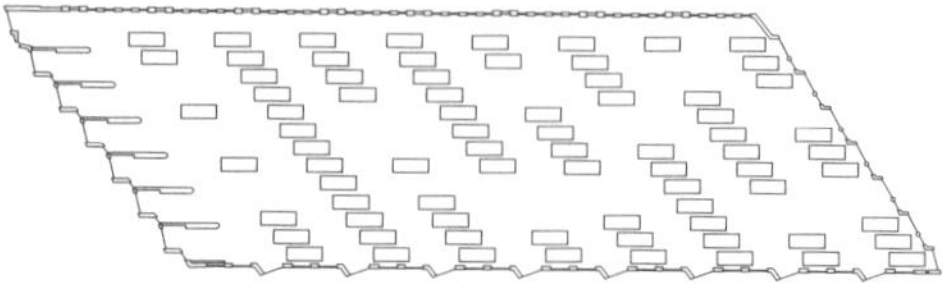

© Denis Esakov

architects
K. Melnikov, V. Shukhov

type
cultural

construction
1926-1927

Chistye Prudy - Sretenka - Prospekt Mira

61. BO 2-M offices
62. Yaroslavsky station
63. Ex-Garage Novo-Ryazanskaya
64. Narkomzem
65. Ministry of Transport
66. NKPS People's Commissariat of Transportation
67. Gostorg
68. Tsentrosoyuz
69. Central Aerohydrodynamic Institute
70. Gazgolder
71. Winzavod
72. Art House
73. Military barracks
74. Taganka Theater

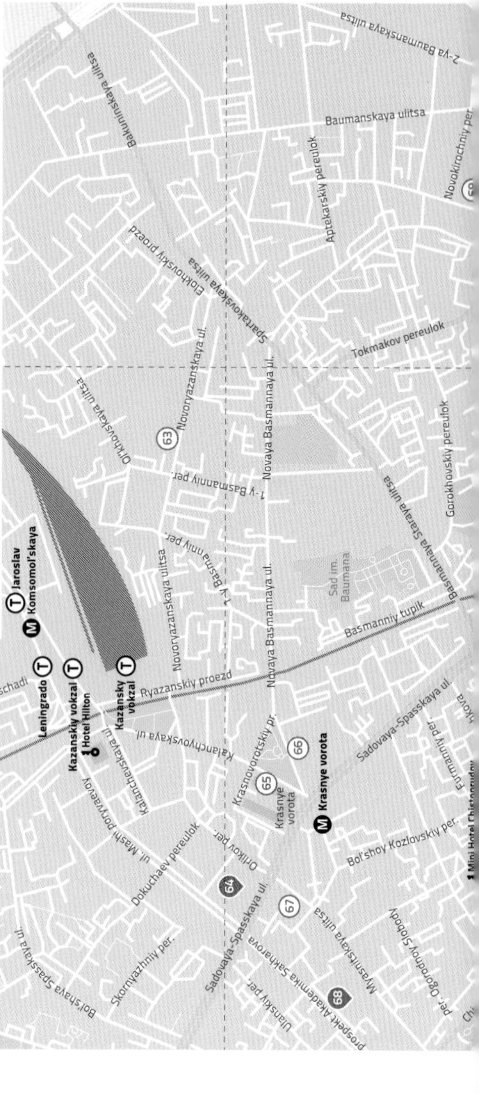

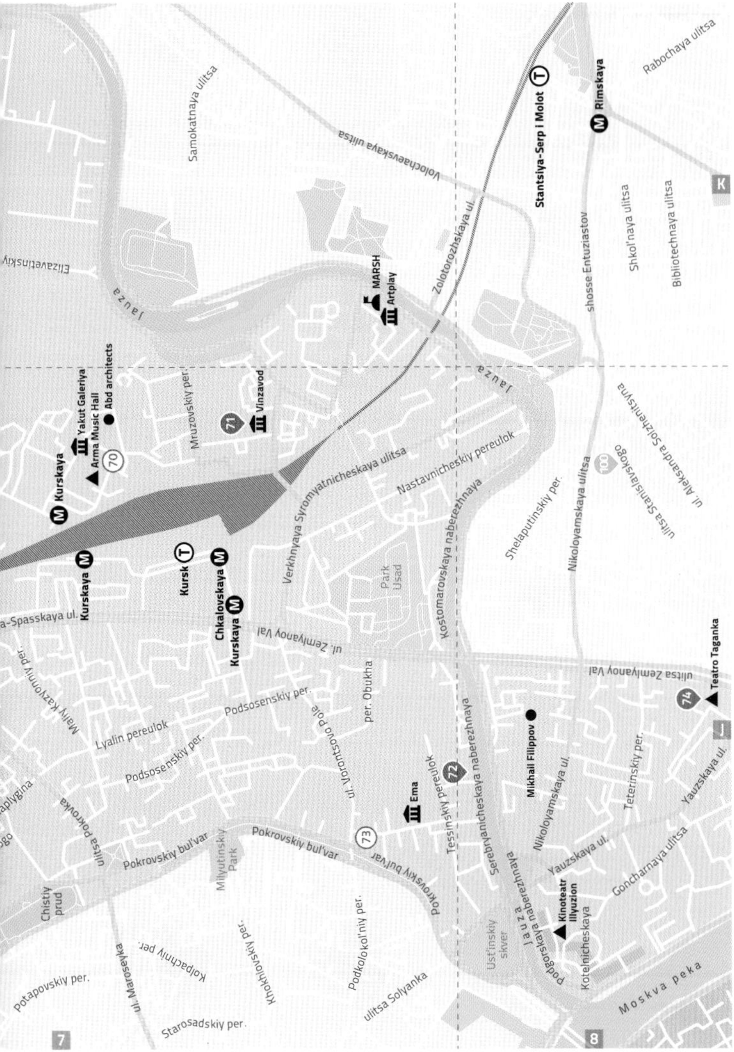
Kurskaya
Yakut Galeriya
Arma Music Hall
Abd architects
70
Kurskaya
Kursk
Chkalovskaya
Kurskaya
Mruzovskiy per.
71
Vinzavod
Samokatnaya ulitsa
Elizavetinskiy
Jauza
Volochaevskaya ulitsa
Zolotorozhskaya ul.
MARSH
Artplay
Stantsiya-Serp i Molot
Rimskaya
Rabochaya ulitsa
shosse Entuziastov
Shkol'naya ulitsa
Bibliotechnaya ulitsa
Verkhnyaya Syromyatnicheskaya ulitsa
Nastavnicheskiy pereulok
Kostomarovskaya naberezhnaya
Park Usad
ul. Zemlyanoy Val
Shelaputinskiy per.
Nikoloyamskaya ulitsa
ulitsa Stanislavskogo
ul. Aleksandra Solzhenitsyna
100
ulitsa Zemlyanoy Val
Teatro Taganka
74
a-Spasskaya ul.
Malyi Kazyonniy per.
Lyalin pereulok
Podsosenskiy per.
Podsosenskiy per.
ul. Vorontsovo Pole
per. Obukha
Tessinskiy pereulok
72
Ema
Serebryanicheskaya naberezhnaya
Mikhail Filippov
Nikoloyamskaya ul.
Teterinskiy per.
Yauzskaya ul.
Yauzskaya ul.
Goncharnaya ulitsa
Kinoteatr Illyuzion
Kotelnicheskaya
Podgorskaya naberezhnaya
Jauza
Ust'inskiy skver
Moskva reka
aplygina
ulitsa Pokrovka
Pokrovskiy bul'var
Pokrovskiy bul'var
Pokrovskiy bul'var
73
Milyutinskiy Park
Chistiy prud
Podkolokol'niy per.
Khokhlovskiy per.
Kolpachniy per.
ul. Maroseyka
Potapovskiy per.
Starosadskiy per.
ulitsa Solyanka
7
8
J
K

61. BO 2-M offices

Shchepkina ulitsa, 61/2
129110 Moscow

10 > Maryina Roshcha;
6 > Rizhskaya

0/12/12a/19/24 >
Olimpiyskiy prospekt;
38 > Ulitsa Shchepkina
- Trifonovskiy khram

The contoured forms of this office tower by the firm Ostozhenka were determined by the unusual and irregular shape of the lot, located at the intersection of ulitsa Trifonovskaya and Orlovsky pereulok. With its sharp concave lines, it looks almost like the bow of the ship that has settled into the urban environment. The building is organized around a vertical circulation core and is supported by a structure that is set far back with respect to the perimeter. Because the structural system is not visible from the exterior, the fully-glazed facade appears as if a curtain stretched across the edges of the floors. The corners are extremely transparent, with an almost immaterial appearance that confers a sense of lightness to the building.
The reflections on the concave surfaces of the facades vary greatly throughout the day and with changing weather patterns.

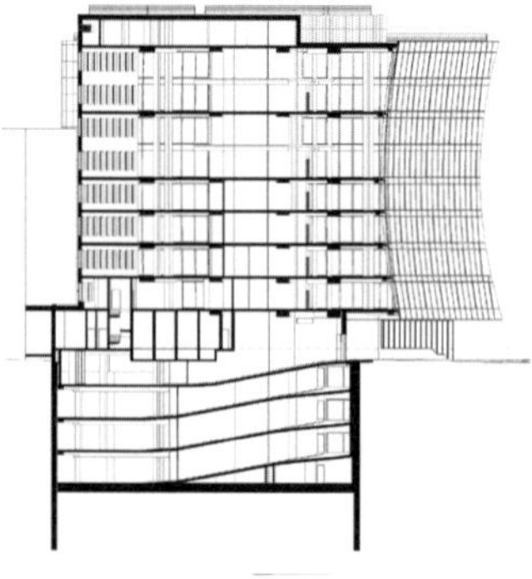

© Ostozhenka

architects
Ostozhenka

type
offices

construction
2010

64. Narkomzem

Sadovaya- Spasskaya ulitsa 11/1
107078 Moscow

external viewing only

www.mcx.ru

1 > Krasnye Vorota

Б > Prospekt Akademika Sakharova;
24 > Krasnye Vorota

This building, located on one of the main arteries of the city, at the intersection between ulitsa Sadovaja Spasskaja and Orlikov pereulok, was designed to house the offices of the People's Commissariat for Agriculture. It presents a clear and masterly example of a certain late "Constructivism," in some ways already mannered and full of monumental emphasis, that appeared in many Soviet cities towards the end of the 1920s and the beginning of the 1930s. The building was designed by Alexey Shchusev (1873-1949). The designer of the Lenin Mausoleum in the Red Square, Shchusev belonged to the generation of masters who trained during the late 19th century at the prestigious School of Fine Arts of St. Petersburg. After working for a certain period in the Russian Modern style (Art Nouveau), he repositioned himself as a complete independent within the sphere of the architectural currents of the 1920s. Though he never adhered to the Constructivist movement, Shchusev clearly understood its message, reinterpreting Constructivist style elements with sculptural sensitivity and a feel for the monumental, particularly readable in his "hinge" solutions that link the various volumes of the imposing Narkomzem building.

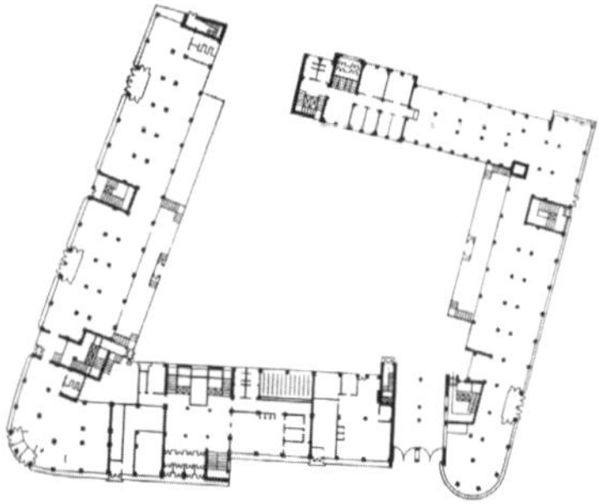

architects
A. Shchusev

type
offices

construction
1928-1933

68. Tsentrosoyuz

Myasnitskaya ulitsa 39
101000 Moscow

external viewing only

+7 (495) 6074087
stat@gks.ru
www.gks.ru

1 > Krasnye Vorota;
6 > Turgenevskaya;
10 > Sretenskiy Bulvar

9 > Maly Kharitonyevsky pereulok

This is one of the major works by Le Corbusier built before World War II. In 1928, the Central Union of Consumer Cooperatives (Tsentrosoyuz) held an open competition, inviting Le Corbusier, among others, to participate. Supported by the avant-garde circles of Moscow, Le Corbusier won the competition and the commission to prepare the final design. A series of substantial changes to the original project led to the final version. The volumes were rearranged, resulting in greater emphasis on the plasticity of the forms. At the same time it solved the problem of integrating the building into a lot that was already defined by pre-existing buildings, still visible today. The facade treatment is characterized by large ribbon windows that alternate with solid masonry surfaces, executed in course-textured blocks of pinkish-brown tuff from Armenia. The vestibule, inserted in the central portion of the main volume, leads to the large ramps that substitute the stairways, linking the work areas to the meeting room and the clubroom.
This Corbusian masterpiece is located near other remarkable buildings, such as the Gostorg by Boris Velikosky and Mikhail Barshch, an example of early constructivism, and the Ministry of Transport building by Ivan Fomin.

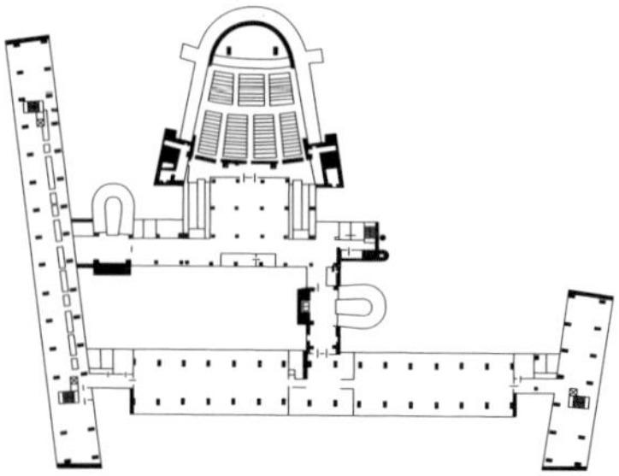

architects
Le Corbusier, P. Jeanneret

type
offices

construction
1928-1937

71. Winzavod

4-y Syromyatnichesky pereulok 1 1/8c6
105120 Moscow

open to public

+7 (495) 9174646
winzavod@winzavod.ru
www.winzavod.ru

24 > 4-y Syromyatnichesky pereulok

3/5 > Kurskaya;
10 > Chkalovskaya

Moskva Kurskaya

40 > Verkhnyaya Syromyatnicheskaya ulitsa

The artist-architect Alexander Brodsky converted this former "wine factory" into a contemporary art center, with a floor area of approximately 18,000 square meters. The project called for the installation of art galleries, artists' studios, design shops, offices, cafés, a restaurant, and a cinema. Located east of the Kurskaya train station, Winzavod is immersed in the typical fabric of the historic industrial suburb, by now completely incorporated into the city by urban expansion. The complex of buildings converted into an art center was built between the late 19th century and the 1960s. The exterior restoration work mainly concerned the facades, which were refinished and repainted brick red, and the window frames, which were replaced with similar wood frames.
Canopies in structural steel and transparent PVC protect the passageways between the buildings, which are arranged around a courtyard with a sculptural fountain in the center.
Even more interesting are the sensible solutions employed by Brodsky for the architectural preservation of the interiors. Particularly evocative are the underground spaces that were originally used as wine cellars.

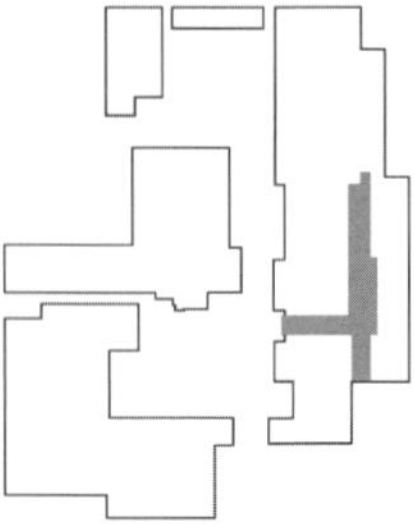

architects	type	construction
A. Brodsky	cultural	2005-2007

72. Art House

Serebryanicheskaya naberezhnaya 19
109028 Moscow

open to public

10 > Chkalovskaya

158 > Yauzskiye Vorota - Pamyatnik Pogranichnikam Otechestva

45/63 > Yauzskye Vorota - Pamyatnik Pogranichnikam Otechestva

Art House is located in a former industrial district that overlooks the north banks of the Yauza River and is rapidly becoming a cultural and artistic center of Moscow.
A multi-functional complex of residences, offices and cultural venues, Art House is articulated in two offset volumes, both square in plan but differing in size. The site was originally occupied by a factory, the memory of which inspired the dominant theme of dark-colored facebrick, the unifying element of the composition.
The apparent and purposeful monotony is belied by the wealth of chromatic shades of brick and resulting plays of light on the surfaces. The smaller volume, a square tower with slightly inclined walls, is darker with respect to the larger, elongated volume that forms the main facade of the complex. The two volumes feature interesting variations in the composition of the facades, determined by the rhythmic patterns of the full-height windows and by the diagonal impost of the roofline.

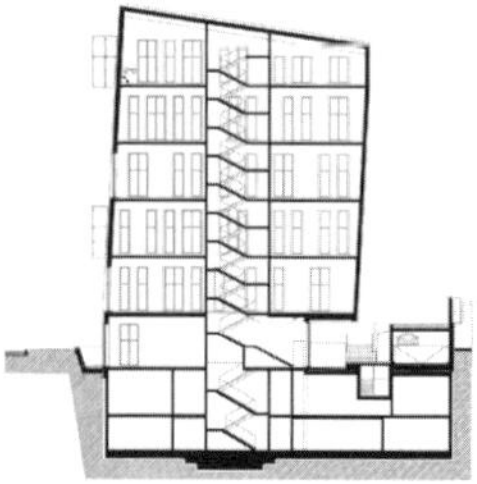

© Sergey Skuratov Architects

architects
Sergey Skuratov Architects

type
multipurpose

construction
2007-2012

74. Taganka Theater

Zemlyanoy Val ulitsa 76/21
109240 Moscow

by appointment

taganka@theatre.ru
taganka.theatre.ru

7 > Taganskaya;
5 > Taganskaya;
8 > Marksistskaya

156 > Taganskaya

16/27/63/63k >
Taganskaya

This theater is one of the more interesting works of architecture from the 1970s-80s, and not just in the Soviet Union. Incorporating and restoring parts of the existing building, the architects brilliantly solved the main project constraint, consisting of a difficult, triangular shaped lot, the narrowest portion of which had to accommodate the backstage areas of the theater complex. The need to accommodate special theatrical staging requirements inspired the concept behind the arrangement of the stage areas and public spaces. With the support of ambitious and innovative technical apparatus, the aim was to achieve an updated vision of "total theater." The building is completely clad in brick, which gives it a strong sense of material expressiveness while allowing it to dialogue with its eclectic surroundings. It appears as a sort of magic box, both magnificent and compact. The composition of the facades, with their rhythmic window openings, intersecting geometries and plays of shadows, brings to mind certain fragments of the most avant-garde works by Konstantin Melnikov, in particular the rear of the Rusakov Workers' Club.

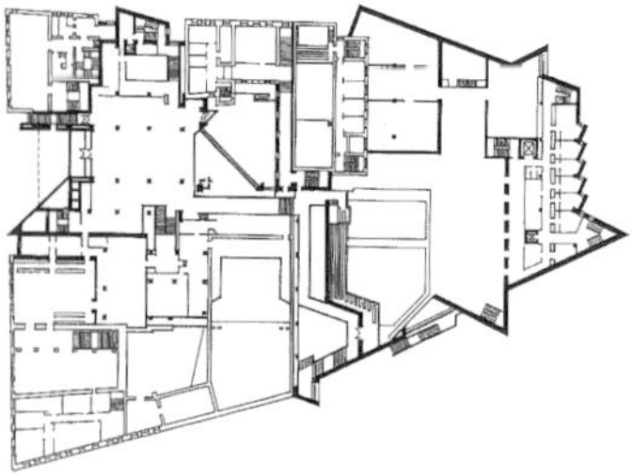

architects
V. Asinimov, Y. Gnedovsky

type
cultural

construction
1973-1985

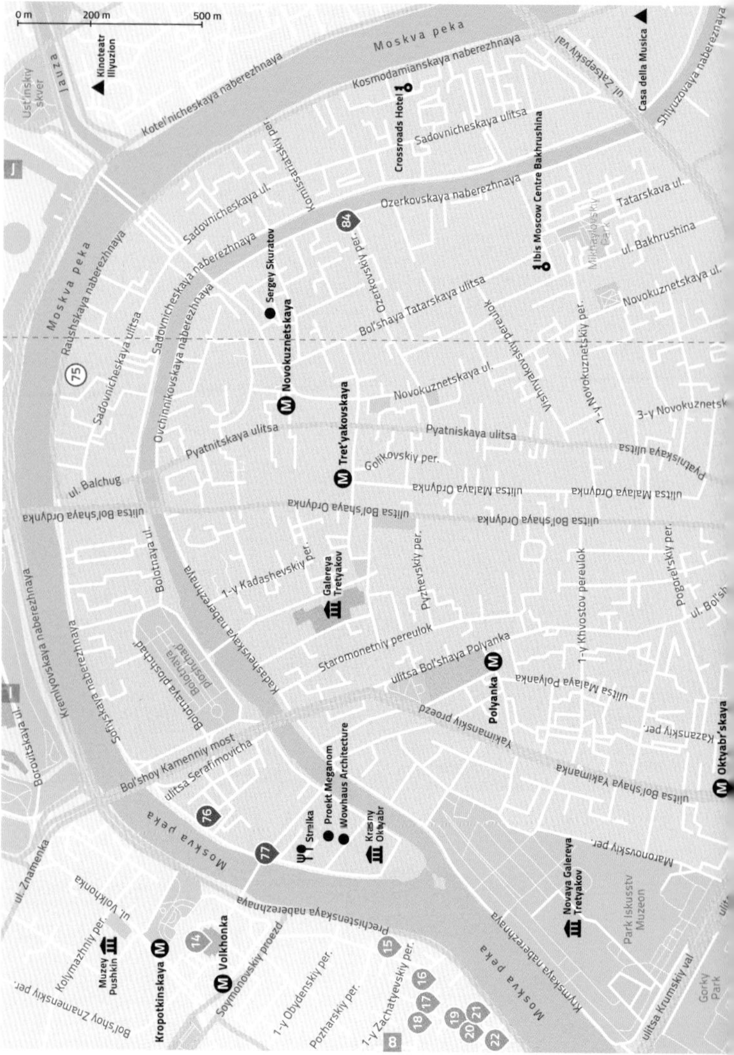

0 m
200 m
500 m
Moskva reka
Jauza
Ust'inskiy skver
Kinoteatr Illyuzion
Kotel'nicheskaya naberezhnaya
Kosmodamianskaya naberezhnaya
ul. Zatsepskiy val
Casa della Musica
Shlyuzovaya naberezhnaya
Crossroads Hotel
Sadovnicheskaya ulitsa
Komissariatskiy per.
Sadovnicheskaya ul.
Ozerkovskaya naberezhnaya
Ibis Moscow Centre Bakhrushina
Tatarskaya ul.
Mikhaylovskiy Park
ul. Bakhrushina
Novokuznetskaya ul.
84
Ozerkovskiy per.
Sergey Skuratov
Novokuznetskaya
Bol'shaya Tatarskaya ulitsa
Vishnyakovskiy pereulok
1-y Novokuznetskiy per.
3-y Novokuznetsk
Raushskaya naberezhnaya
Sadovnicheskaya naberezhnaya
Ovchinnikovskaya naberezhnaya
Sadovnicheskaya ulitsa
75
Novokuznetskaya ul.
Tret'yakovskaya
Pyatnitskaya ulitsa
Pyatniskaya ulitsa
Golikovskiy per.
ul. Balchug
ulitsa Malaya Ordynka
ulitsa Bol'shaya Ordynka
Bolotnaya ul.
1-y Kadashevskiy per.
Galereya Tretyakov
Pyzhevskiy per.
Pogorel'skiy per.
ul. Bol'sh
1-y Khvostov pereulok
Staromonetniy pereulok
ulitsa Bol'shaya Polyanka
Polyanka
ulitsa Malaya Polyanka
Kremlyovskaya naberezhnaya
Sofiyskaya naberezhnaya
Bolotnaya ploshchad'
Kadashevskaya naberezhnaya
Yakimanskiy proezd
Kazanskiy per.
Oktyabr'skaya
Borovitskaya ul.
Bol'shoy Kamenniy most
ulitsa Serafimovicha
ulitsa Bol'shaya Yakimanka
76
77
Strelka
Proekt Meganom
Wowhaus Architecture
Krasny Oktyabr
Maronovskiy per.
ul. Znamenka
ul. Volkhonka
Kolymazhniy per.
Muzey Pushkin
Kropotkinskaya
14
Volkhonka
Prechistenskaya naberezhnaya
Soymonovskiy proezd
15
1-y Obydenskiy per.
Pozharskiy per.
1-y Zachatyevskiy per.
16
17
18
19
20
21
22
Krymskaya naberezhnaya
Novaya Galereya Tretyakov
Park Iskusstv Muzeon
Gorky Park
ulitsa Krumskiy val
Bol'shoy Znamenskiy per.

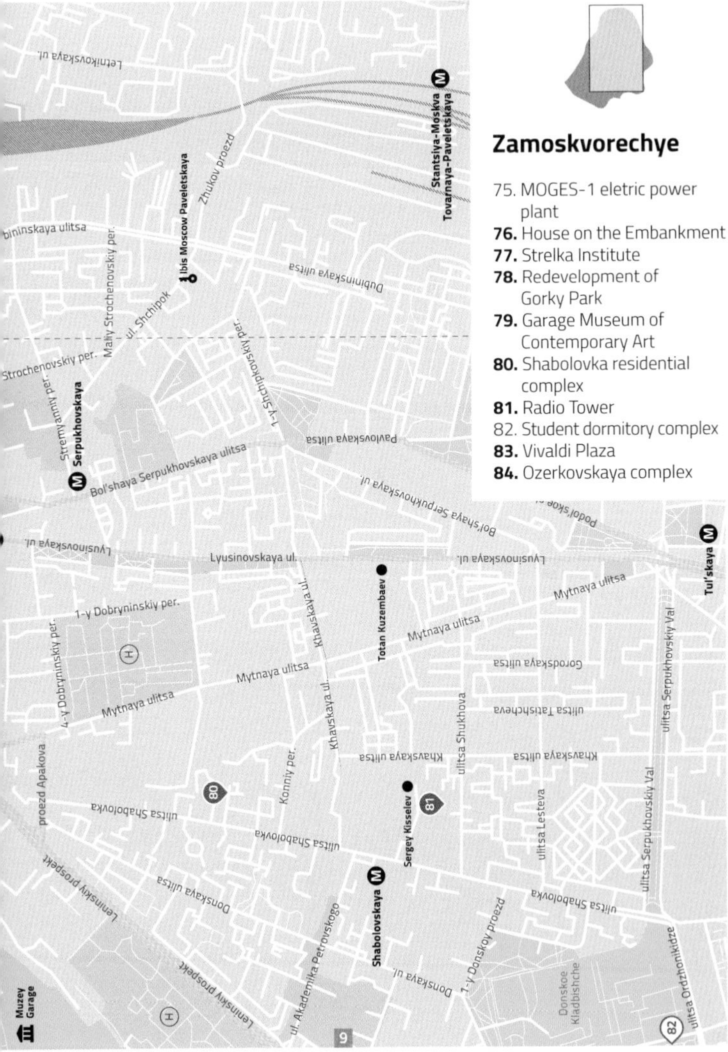

Zamoskvorechye

75. MOGES-1 eletric power plant
76. House on the Embankment
77. Strelka Institute
78. Redevelopment of Gorky Park
79. Garage Museum of Contemporary Art
80. Shabolovka residential complex
81. Radio Tower
82. Student dormitory complex
83. Vivaldi Plaza
84. Ozerkovskaya complex

76. House on the Embankment

ulitsa Serafimovicha 2/20
119072 Moscow

January - December
Tue - Wed - Fri /
10 am - 6.30 pm
Thu / 11 am - 9 pm
Sat - Sun / 11 am - 6 pm
Mon / closed

+7 (495) 9594936
museumdom@yandex.ru
www.museumdom.narod.ru

1 > Kropotkinskaya;
9 > Borovitskaya

6/K > Kinoteatr Udarnik

1/1k/4/33/62 > Kinoteatr Udarnik

This gigantic building, one of the first true residential megastructures of the twentieth century and one of the most important experimental building projects realized in Moscow in the late 1920s, was immortalized by a famous novel by Jury Trifonov, *House on the Embankment*. Built to house the Soviet ruling class, many of whom were later victims of the Stalinist purges in the late 1930s, the complex was often held as an example for reconstruction projects in central Moscow.
It was, in fact, a veritable citadel of articulated volumes, containing every sort of convenience and amenity to meet the lifestyle demands of its select population of inhabitants: a restaurant, a cinema and theater with a telescopic roof for open-air performances during the summer season, shops, and childcare facilities. The architect, Boris Iofan, had also trained in Rome. In his approach to the project, which dates to the end of the 1920s, he probably took into account the construction of the (never-built) Palace of the Soviets, which was meant to replace the Cathedral of Christ the Saviour on the opposite bank of the river. Iofan was, in fact, one of the instigators of the competition and participated in the final design.

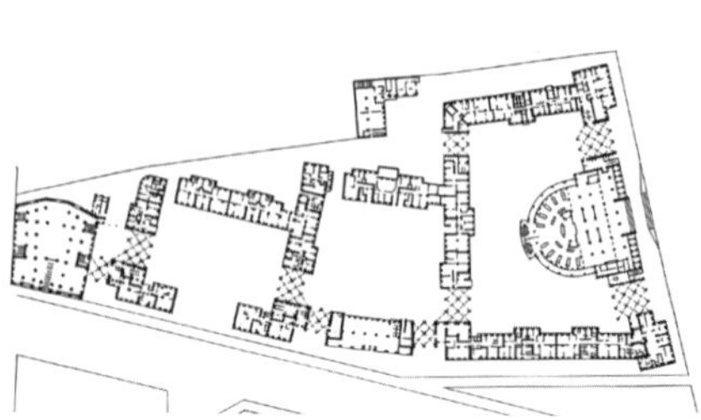

architects
B. Iofan

type
multifunctional complex

construction
1927-1931

77. Strelka Institute

Bersenevskaya naberezhnaya 14
119072 Moscow

open to public

+7 (495) 2680619
more@strelka.com
www.strelka.com

1 > Kropotkinskaya;
9 > Borovitskaya

6/K > Kinoteatr Udarnik

1/1k/4/33/62 > Kinoteatr Udarnik

This interesting and unique space, currently one of the city's most fashionable cultural magnets, was designed by the Wowhaus architecture firm of Moscow. It is situated on a portion of the centrally located and picturesque island of Bolotnaya, created by a fork in the Moscova River, on the site of a former chocolate factory, the splendid and acclaimed Krasny Oktyabr or Red October. The building and adjacent public space provide good views of the redeveloped Ostozhenko district and the reconstructed Cathedral of Christ the Saviour, which is linked to the island by a recently built footbridge with a decidedly eclectic style. The complex gravitates around the Strelka Institute for Media, Architecture and Design, promoted by wealthy Russian entrepreneurs under the cultural inspiration of Rem Koolhaas. It includes a lively bar-bistrot with a crowd-drawing terrace, as well as a large open space, formed by two amphitheaters, one opposite the other, which hosts a variety of activities, including lessons and readings, film screenings, yoga classes, and many other events.

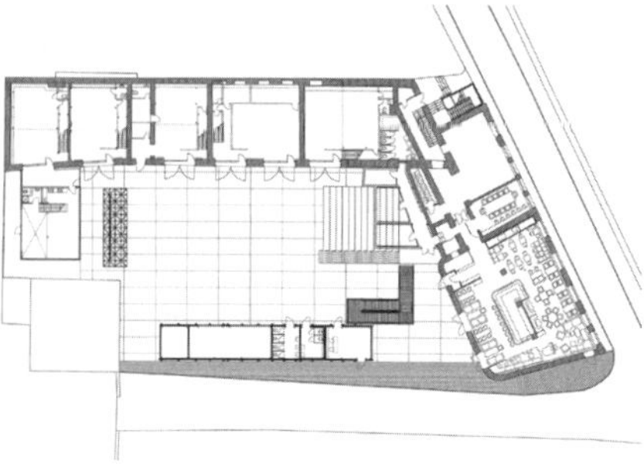

© Wowhaus

architects
Wowhaus

type
cultural

construction
2009-2010

78. Redevelopment of Gorky Park

Krymsky Val ulitsa 9
119049 Moscow

open to public

+7 (045) 9950020
info@park-gorkogo.com
www.park-gorkogo.com

1/5 > Park Kultury;
5/6 > Oktyabrskaya

111/196 > Gorodskaya bolnitsa № 1

4/7/33/33K/62/84 > Gorodskaya bolnitsa № 1;
Б/10/Бк > TsPKiO imeni Gorkogo;
4/33/62 > Oktyabrskaya

Gorky Park is Moscow's principle urban recreational area. Conceived in the 1930s, it is part of the integrated system of green spaces "for culture and repose," the design of which involved many of the great architects of the times, including Konstantin Melnikov and Moisei Ginzburg, as well as Aleksandr Vlasov in its final layout (1934-36).
The park has recently undergone major redevelopment as part of an effort by the city of Moscow to improve the quality of its public spaces. It has become one of the main themes of the new course of the city.
Among the projects worth special note are the refined renovations of many of the park's outdoor areas — the skating rink, the open-air cinema, the pavilions, the pergola, Golitsynsky Pond, Olive Beach, and the Krymskaya Embankment — all by the Muscovite firm Wowhaus, which was founded in 2007 by Oleg Shapiro and Dimitri Likin.

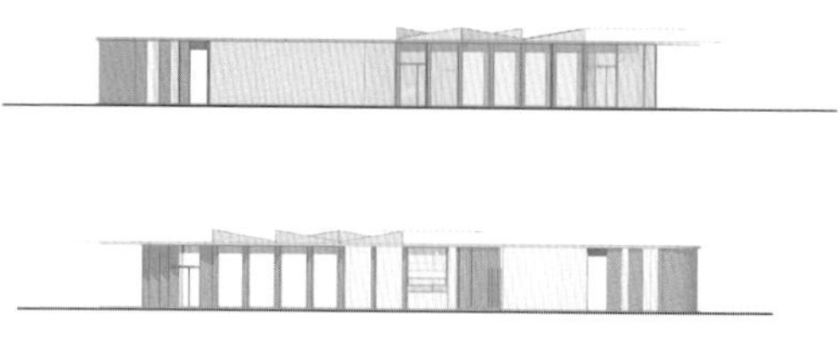

architects
K. Melnikov, M. Ginzburg,
A. Vlasov
Wowhaus

type
riverside park

construction
1923-1955

2013

79. Garage Museum of Contemporary Art

Krymsky Val ulitsa 9
119049 Moscow

Mon - Sun / 11 am - 10 pm

garagemca.org

1/5 > Park Kultury;
5/6 > Oktyabrskaya

111/196 > Gorodskaya bolnitsa № 1

4/7/33/33K/62/84 > Gorodskaya bolnitsa № 1;
4/33/62 > Oktyabrskaya

The Garage Museum was founded in 2008 and was previously hosted in the Bakhmetevsky Bus Garage by Konstantin Melnikov. The museum has now found a permanent home in Gorky Park, following the completion of an adaptive reuse project by the firm OMA of a prefabricated Soviet pavilion from the 1960s, which was originally designed as an entertainment venue for the working classes.
The project for the conversion of the building into a center for exhibitions and cultural activities involved wrapping it in a translucent polycarbonate skin. The structural system and some of the original decorative elements were preserved.
The double-layered membrane, a characteristic feature of the project, is raised 2.25 m with respect to the ground level, offering good views of the park, concealing the structure and building systems, and providing a surface that can be used for projections or graphic communications.
The entrances are marked by two huge movable walls that slide vertically, thereby freeing up the central area and permitting the passage of large artworks.

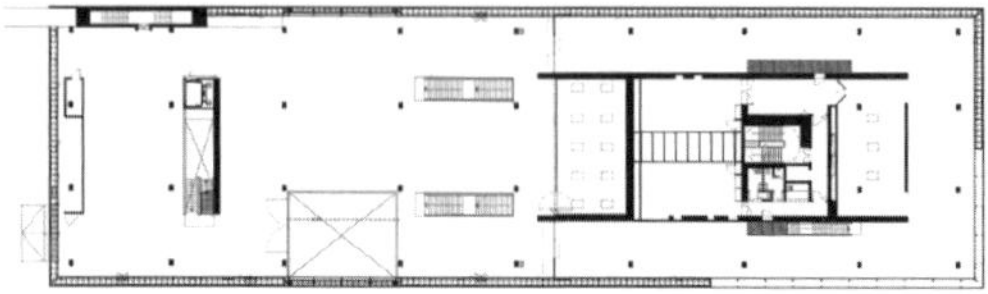

architects
OMA

type
cultural

construction
2012-2014

80. Shabolovka residential complex

Shabolovka ulitsa 23
119049 Moscow

external viewing only

14/26/47/A > Fabrika Udarnitsa

5/6 > Oktyabrskaya;
6 > Shabolovskaya

111/196 > Kaluzhskaya ploshchad

4/62 > Oktyabrskaya;
7/33k/84 > Kaluzhskaya ploshchad

These three residential towers by the firm Ostozhenka are an imposing presence in their neighborhood, the historic Shabolovka district in Moscow's southern outskirts, near Vladimir Shukhov's famous radio tower and several notable examples of early Soviet-era housing projects. These include, from the second half of the 1920s, the Communal House designed by Georgy Vol'fenzon (with others), and the housing development by Nikolai Travin, with its original layout. Distinguishing features of the towers are the interesting arrangement of the volumes on the irregularly-shaped lot, the large cornices which unify the composition, and the color gradations of the facades which instead help to differentiate the three buildings.
The design solution was a response to the constraints imposed by the shape of the lot, the surrounding buildings, the sun exposure, and lighting regulations.
The complex was also arranged in such a way as not to interfere, in terms of urban landscape, with the Church of the Holy Trinity.

architects
Ostozhenka

type
residential

construction
2001-2004

81. Radio Tower

Shukhova ulitsa 8
115162 Moscow

external viewing only

14/26/47/A > Shabolovskaya

6 > Shabolovskaya

10 > Shukhova ulitsa

This unique and monumental structure, with its lacy silhouette, was the symbol of Soviet radio for many decades and a landmark of the new Socialist Moscow. Contemporary to Tatlin's famous Monument to the Third International, the project originated from a provision by the Soviet Government for the installation in Moscow of, "in the very near future, a broadcast station with the most modern equipment and materials," in order to ensure communications between the USSR and the Western capital cities.
The first solution, developed by the engineer Vladimir G. Shukhov (1853-1939), called for a 350-meter tall structure, which would have made it higher than the Eiffel Tower.
The version that was actually built, at 150 m tall, was more commensurate to the financial means of the emerging Soviet nation. Fascinating for its lightness and simplicity, the structure consists of a series of hyperboloids that generate a conical form.

architects
V. Shukhov

type
infrastructural

construction
1919-1922

83. Vivaldi Plaza

Letnikovskaya ulitsa 2
115114 Moscow

external viewing only

35/38 > Kozhevnicheskaya ulitsa

2/5 > Paveletskaya

Paveletsky vokzal

13/106/158/632 > Kozhevnicheskaya ulitsa

Vivaldi Plaza is a business center in Paveletsky, an industrial zone currently undergoing a process of transformation. Designed by Sergey Kisselev, its layout recalls that of a fortress. The four office buildings and the hotel are distributed around an interior courtyard, forming a sort of perimeter wall that also evokes the kvartal, a typical of urban construction in Moscow in the 1930s. This arrangement helps create an environment that is protected from the center's chaotic and harshly eclectic surroundings. The site is adjacent to one of Moscow's major traffic nodes linking to Domodedovo Airport. The inner courtyard also acts as a compositional and functional focal point, with a hill garden, restaurants and shops at the ground-floor levels. The upper floors are devoted to office space.
The theme of transparency of the building envelope is resolved by means of cladding systems that differentiate between the exterior facades and those facing the courtyard. The uniformly mirrored surface of the exterior facades functions almost like a double skin over the brown curtain wall of the base and sides. In stark contrast, the incisive rhythmic composition of the interior facades breaks up the large volumes and gives them a sense of proportion.

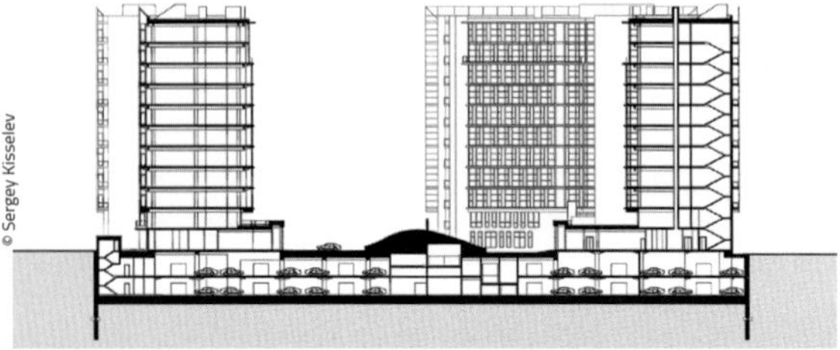

© Sergey Kisselev

© Sergey Kisselev

architects
S. Kisselev

type
offices

construction
2004-2012

84. Ozerkovskaya complex

Ozerkovskaya naberezhnaya 22
115184 Moscow

external viewing only

3/39/A > Tretyakovskaya

2 > Novokuznetskaya; **6/8** > Tretyakovskaya

This mixed-use complex was designed by the Muscovite firm SPEECH (Tchoban & Kuznetsov). The area on which it is built was initially regulated by a redevelopment plan that provided for the construction of office buildings and an apartment hotel. Though it was later decided not to include the northeast part of the island in the new redevelopment plan, the architects decided to follow the guidelines of the previous plan in their design of this multipurpose complex.
The compositional solution centers on the creation of a curved pedestrian street, starting from the embankment, with the group of four buildings organized around it. Shops, cafés and restaurants all along the ground level of the pedestrian street are open to anyone who wishes to take a break or stop and enjoy a view of the river.
The architecture seems to hybridize the legacy of Soviet Neoclassicim, as developed by the architect Ivan Fomin, who spent most of his working life in Leningrad, and certain recent works in Germany that have undoubtedly influenced the architect, Sergei Tchoban, who was born in St. Petersburg but established himself professionally in Germany.

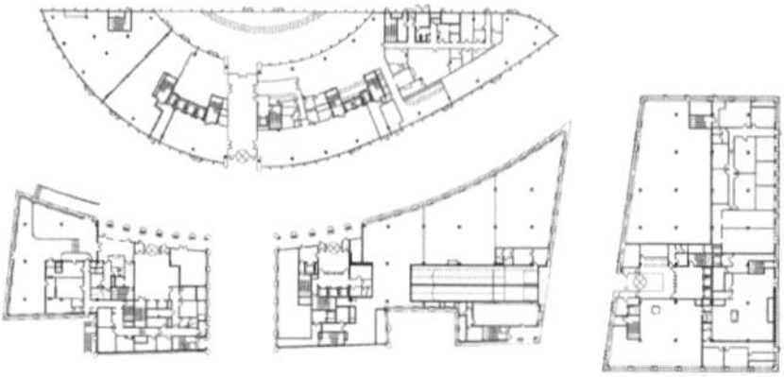

© SPEECH

architects
SPEECH

type
offices

construction
2005-2011

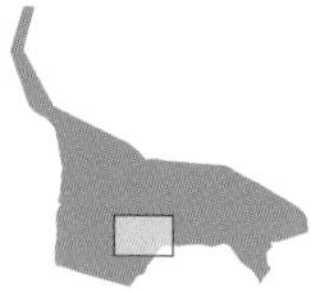

North

85. Central Dynamo Stadium
86. Mercedes-Benz Plaza
87. Siemens AG
88. Aerobus residential complex
89. Alcon
90. Metropolis
91. Metro AG
92. Khimki-IKEA
93. Aeroflot headquarters
94. VDNKh Tower
95. VDNKh
96. Ostankino Tower
97. Monument to the Conquerors of Space
98. Burevestnik Workers' Club
99. Rusakov Workers' Club

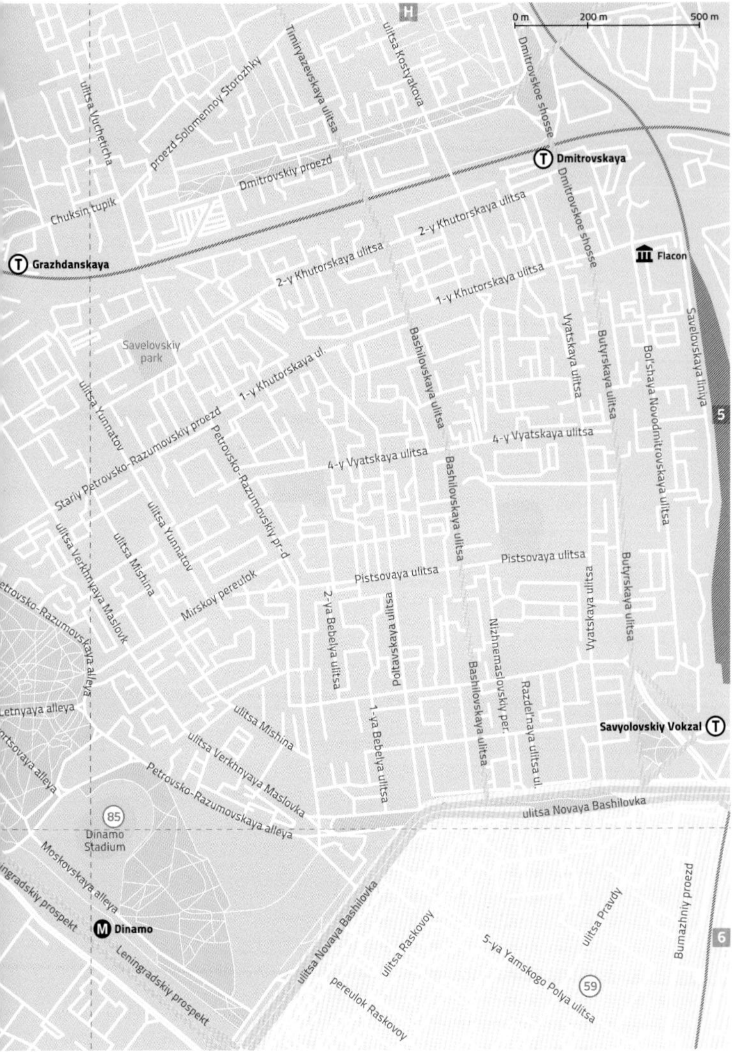
0 m
200 m
500 m
H
ulitsa Vuchetich
proezd Solomennoy Storozhky
Timiryazevskaya ulitsa
ulitsa Kostyakova
Dmitrovskoe shosse
Dmitrovskaya
Dmitrovskiy proezd
Chuksin tupik
Grazhdanskaya
2-y Khutorskaya ulitsa
1-y Khutorskaya ulitsa
Flacon
Savelovskiy park
1-y Khutorskaya ul.
Vyatskaya ulitsa
Butyrskaya ulitsa
Bol'shaya Novodmitrovskaya ulitsa
Savelovskaya liniya
5
Bashilovskaya ulitsa
4-y Vyatskaya ulitsa
ulitsa Yunnatov
Stariy Petrovsko-Razumovskiy proezd
Petrovsko-Razumovskiy pr-d
ulitsa Verkhnyaya Maslovk
ulitsa Mishina
Mirskoy pereulok
Pistsovaya ulitsa
2-ya Bebelya ulitsa
Poltavskaya ulitsa
Nizhnemaslovskiy per.
Razdel'naya ulitsa ul.
Petrovsko-Razumovskaya alleya
Letnyaya alleya
Portsovaya alleya
1-ya Bebelya ulitsa
ulitsa Verkhnyaya Maslovka
Savyolovskiy Vokzal
ulitsa Novaya Bashilovka
85
Dinamo Stadium
Moskovskaya alleya
Leningradskiy prospekt
Dinamo
ulitsa Raskovoy
pereulok Raskovoy
5-ya Yamskogo Polya ulitsa
ulitsa Pravdy
59
Bumazhniy proezd
6

86. Mercedes-Benz Plaza

Leningradsky prospekt 39c42
125167 Moscow

external viewing only

2 > Aeroport, Dinamo

105 > Sportivny kompleks TsSKA

6/12/43/65/70/82 > Sportivny kompleks TsSKA

Designed by the firm ABD architects, this building is located in the northwest administrative district, near the TSSCA sports complex and Leningradsky prospekt. The building consists of two volumes. The first is an elongated, two-floor structure facing directly onto Leningradsky prospekt. The second is a nine-floor tower situated over the first volume, approximately triangular in plan, with a rounded front facade.
The low volume relates directly to the street and to the public. It hosts the Mercedes-Benz exhibition space, a restaurant and offices. The glazed facades permit views of the interior exhibition spaces while at the same time projecting the automobile showroom out towards the street. The executive offices are distributed in the tower around a concave atrium which communicates directly with the showroom spaces, in this way linking together all of the elements of the building.
The facades were decorated in keeping with the stylistic elements of DaimlerChrysler, as were the interiors, by IKS Hochtief-Frankfurt.

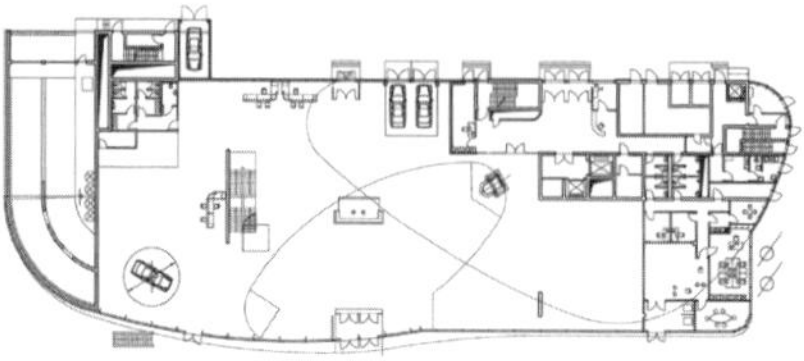

architects
ABD architects

type
offices

construction
2003-2005

87. Siemens AG

Leningradsky prospekt 39
125167 Moscow

external viewing only

2 > Aeroport

6/12/43/65/70/82
> Ulitsa Konstantina Simonova

105 > Ulitsa Konstantina Simonova

The Leningradsky Towers office complex, designed by the German firm Eller + Eller, is situated on the Leningradsky prospekt, one of the principal arteries linking to the center of Moscow. With the construction of numerous business parks, this north-west thoroughfare has become a catalyst of the recent expansion of the service sector.
The project combines the headquarters of Siemens and Sistema-Hals in a rationally designed complex consisting of two office towers, each square in plan, with 35m × 35m sides and approximately 1200 sq m floor area per level. The two 27-floor towers, for a total height of 110 m, are served by independent double-height lobbies. They are situated at opposite corners of a rectangular five-floor volume that forms a sort of plinth containing a large atrium and various shared facilities, including a restaurant-cafeteria and conference and meeting rooms.
The underground levels are devoted to parking and plant rooms.
The complex is labeled "Class A" for energy efficiency and has a total surface area of approximately 105,000 sq m.

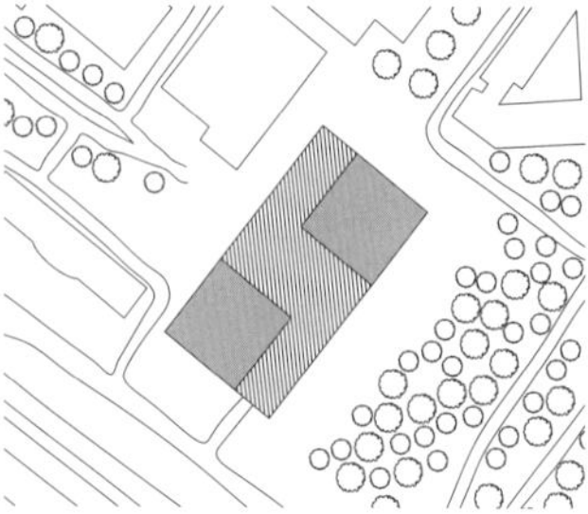

architects
Eller + Eller Architekten

type
offices

construction
2006-2010

88. Aerobus residential complex

Kochnovsky proezd 4к2
125319 Moscow

external viewing only

2 > Aeroport

Grazhdanskaya

105/105k > Ulitsa Akademika Ilyushina;
22/77 > Grazhdanskaya

The Aerobus residential complex is an extreme interpretation of a historic theme of Soviet-era residential design which is still relevant today, the megalith housing block. In this project, Vladimir Plotkin makes no attempt to hide the dimensions of the buildings. Instead, their imposing forms are exalted by means of clarity of layout, integrity of form and repetition of compositional elements. The rhythmic articulation of the fenestration gives readability and proportions to the extraordinary dimensions of the buildings, which are dramatically evident in contrast with their surroundings. The facade is organized into a grid pattern, with the windows of the apartment units grouped in individual quadrants.
The facade pattern progresses into larger modules at the upper levels of the building, emphasizing its crown and correcting possible distortions of perspective when viewed from up close.

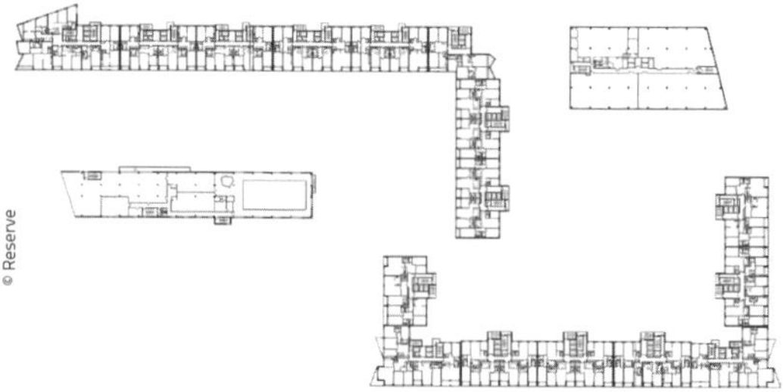

© Reserve

architects
Reserve

type
residential

construction
2005-2007

89. Alcon

Leningradsky prospekt 72
125315 Moscow

external viewing only

2 > Sokol

105/904 > Sokol

6/12/43/70/82/86
> Sokol

The master plan of this business center is by Fitzroy Robinson Architects. The four building volumes, each square in plan, are arranged at the corners of the lot, thereby creating a cross-shaped exterior distribution pattern at the ground level.
The firm ADM completed the architecture with the stipulation that they would not modify the forms of the previously delineated volumes.
Thus the architects concentrated on the facades, which were originally meant to be in white porcelain tiles in a grille pattern. They completely transformed the appearance of the complex by means of tall windows, two modules wide, offset by one module at alternating floors and spaced by terracotta cladding that evokes the brick-red color of the surrounding Soviet-era buildings.
The upper floors, stepped back from the edge, are resolved by a facade system mainly in glass, with very slender horizontal and vertical terracotta elements. This solution lightens the forms and permitted the creation of wood-covered terraces with lawns that serve as mini-parks looking over the city.
Careful attention was also paid to the design of the exterior environment between the buildings. The pedestrian streets are paved in gray granite in quadrant patterns, delineated by strips in black stone with alternating luminous inserts and punctuated by tree planters with seating.

© ADM

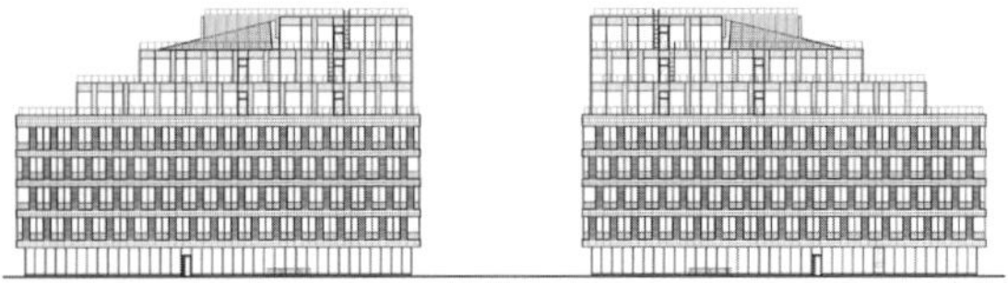

architects
ADM

type
offices

construction
2010-2012

90. Metropolis

Leningradskoye shosse 16Ac2
125171 Moscow

external viewing only

6/27/30 >
Voykovskaya

2 > Voykovskaya

90/114/179/204/780
> Voykovskaya

57 > Voykovskaya

Metropolis is one of the largest multifunctional complexes built in recent years in Moscow. Its vast site was previously occupied by a factory which fell into disuse. It was later converted into temporary commercial spaces and was eventually demolished, in keeping with a widespread pattern of development in post-Soviet Moscow. This new urban space was designed with the aim of becoming a center of attraction on the model of numerous analogous commercial operations based on the importation of experimental schemes and international standards. Thus an elevated square was built as a public gathering place delimited by two distinct groups of buildings. Each of the groups is characterized, in terms of form and volume, by very different solutions which reflect their different functions and symbolic presence. A large shopping center contains a hypermarket, 250 shops, cafés, restaurants, a recreation area and a cinema, while three compact buildings in succession, in energy class A, are devoted to office spaces.

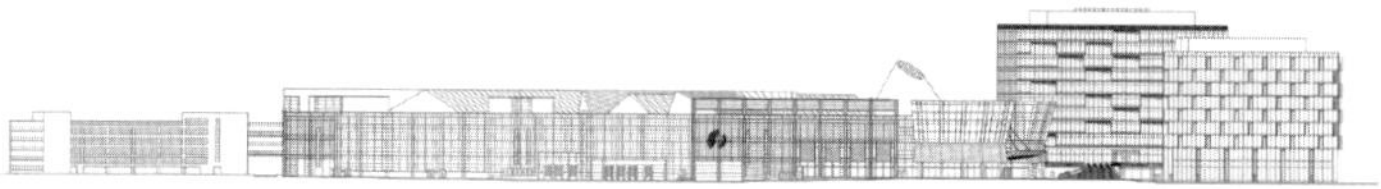

© ABD architects

architects
ABD architects

type
offices

construction
2006-2009

91. Metro AG

Leningradskoye shosse 71
125445 Moscow

external viewing only

173/199/851 >
Khimkinskaya bolnitsa i profilaktory

Metro AG is one of the world's largest retail chains. The group's exponential growth in Russia, in correspondence to the considerable increase in income and demand that have taken place in recent years, made it necessary to open a new representative office in Moscow. Designed by the German firm Eller + Eller Architekten, the complex accommodates 700 employees and is situated at a strategic point in the city, equidistant from the Sheremetevo airport and the center of Moscow, in close proximity to the Moskva River.
The two buildings of the complex, parallel but offset, share a full-height atrium that houses the vertical distribution systems. The ground floor hosts group functions, including an auditorium, a restaurant-café, and meeting rooms. At the upper floors the offices are differentiated by size and organizational layout, ranging from individual offices, small groups of offices, and open-plan areas, according to requirements.
There is space for 100 automobiles at the partially underground parking level.

© Eller + Eller Architekten

architects
Eller + Eller Architekten

type
offices

construction
2004-2007

92. Khimki-IKEA

Leningradskaya ulitsa 39
141401 Moscow

external viewing only

400-з/817/851/905 >
23-y Kilometr

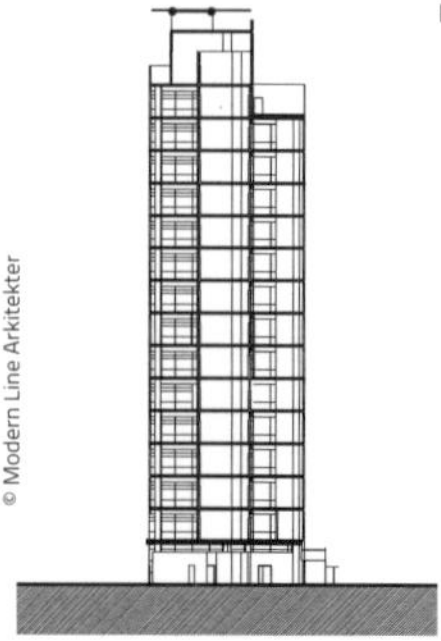

© Modern Line Arkitekter

This office complex is situated in a strategic position between the Sheremetevo airport and the center of Moscow, in an area where IKEA had initially planned to develop a new location.
With the evolution of the program, the home furnishings store was built on the opposite side of the street, and the site was converted into a business park, complete with offices, a hotel, shops, and services.
The master plan is by the firm Chernikhov, while the buildings are by the Swedish firm Modern Line Arkitekter.
The original project provided for six equal parallel buildings, their facades in progressively different colors from building to building, ranging from black to dark blue and finally white, surrounded by a park and a reflecting pond.
Only two of the buildings have been erected, each 15 stories high, for a total floor area of 21,500 sq m.
The fully-glazed facades are clad with transparent and opaque glass panels which reproduce barcode patterns and permit diversification of the interior illumination levels.
The narrow front ends of the buildings, facing onto the main street, are inclined outwards 9 degrees, giving the volumes a dynamic appearance.

architects
Modern Line Arkitekter

type
offices

construction
2013

93. Aeroflot headquarters

Mezhdunarodnoye shosse 31
141425 Moscow

external viewing only

817/851 > Melkisarovo

The Aeroflot headquarters is located immediately adjacent to the Moscow-Sheremetyevo international airport. The building complex communicates a strong corporate image, its forms reiterating the lines of the Russian national airline's winged logo.
Two narrow, parallel six-story volumes, staggered in plan, are united by a full-height glass atrium which houses the vertical circulation and is crossed by walkways connecting the various floors.
The shared atrium space is topped by a skylight roof, resulting in a large greenhouse microclimate that serves the entire complex.
The architectural interpretation of the Aeroflot logo generated the defining visual feature of the complex, the swooping diagonal ends of the two longitudinal volumes.
The ground floor houses the reception and the communication and group functions, while the upper floors are devoted to offices, almost all of which in open-space configurations.
With the exception of white reveals marking the various floors, the facades are fully glazed to a mirror finish that reflects weather conditions and "paints" the building against the sky.

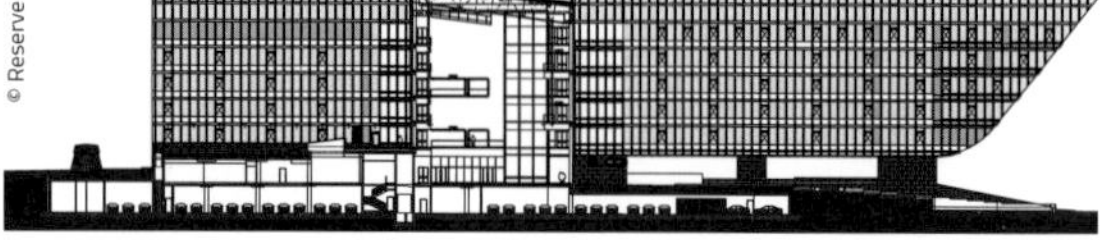

architects
Reserve

type
offices

construction
2004-2010

94. VDNKh Tower

Selskokhozyaystvennaya ulitsa 16
129226 Moscow

external viewing only

6 > VDNKh;
6 > Botanicheskiy Sad

33 > 2-y Selskokhozyaystvenny proezd

48 > 2-y Selskokhozyaystvenny proezd

The tripartite structure of the VDNKh tower stands 35 stories high. Combining the spirit and tradition of Russian rationalism, it acts as a landmark in the northern part of the city. Impressive in size yet well-proportioned, the building brings an additional incisive focal point to an area in the city's periphery whose main reference point is the 540 m Ostankino television and radio tower (1960-1967), a masterpiece of Soviet engineering and a clear tribute, at the height of the space race and the Cold War, to the missile technology of the Soviet Union.
The initial plans for the VDNKh Tower provided for a building of more modest proportions, so as to not exceed the 20-floor maximum height of the buildings already present in the area, in order to conform to the surrounding context. After further analysis, the architects made the building taller, justifying their decision by the fact that the tower would take on the role of focal point as viewed from both the surrounding streets and the center of Moscow, thereby giving the neighborhood a different urban status.

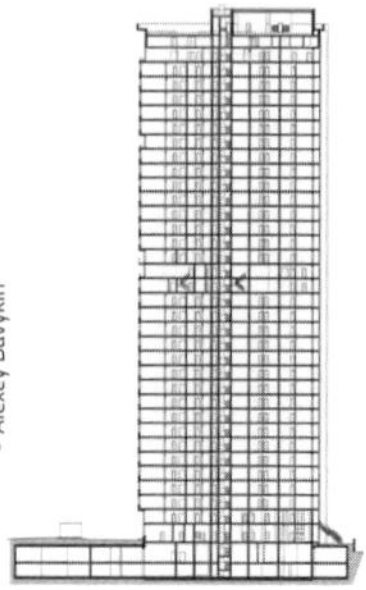

© Alexey Bavykin

architects
A. Bavykin

type
residential

construction
2002-2006

95. VDNKh

Prospekt Mira 119
129223 Moscow

open to public

+7 (495) 5443400
info@vvcentre.ru
www.vvcentre.ru

11/17 > VDNKh

6 > VDNKh, Alekseevskaya

M1 > Vystavochny Tsentr

76/154/239/803 > VDNKh;
56/76/93/136/195/803 > VDNKh Severnaya;
33/154/239/244/834 > VDNKh Yuzhnaya

13/15/36/69/73
VDNKh Yuzhnaya

This exhibition complex was originally built in the northern limits of the city during the mid-1930s as a temporary park for the All-Union Agricultural Exhibition. Following a competition that attracted important architects, artists and sculptors, it was transformed and expanded (between 1937-39 and the postwar period) with new spaces and permanent pavilions, giving it the monumental character that remains today. The original complex, inaugurated in the fall of 1937, was designed by Vyacheslav Oltarzhevsky, whose references to the Art Deco style were severely criticized.
Having reopened at the end of World War II, renovations were successively made to bring it in line with the ideological developments and architectural ideals in terms of esthetics and urban planning that dominated during the late Stalinist era. They are exemplified by the main monumental entrance (I. Melchanov) inspired by the Brandenburg Gate, and the Pavilion by Y. Shchuko — an obvious homage to St. Petersburg classicism (the Admiralty building) — that forms its background. In the second half of the 1950s, the complex underwent further transformation, involving the construction or reconstruction of a number of pavilions in the modernist style imposed by Khrushchev.

© Umberto Zanetti

architects
various architects

type
exhibition grounds

construction
1937-1954

99. Rusakov Workers' Club

Stromynka ulitsa 6
107014 Moscow

external viewing only

4Л/7/13/33 >
Babaevskaya ulitsa

1 > Sokolniki

78/265/716 >
Babaevskaya ulitsa

14/32/41 >
Babaevskaya ulitsa

Between 1927 and 1929, Konstantin Melnikov designed numerous workers' clubs, each very different from the others, both in terms of interior layout and formal investigation. The most famous of these is the Rusakov Workers' Club.
The interior is flexibly articulated. The main auditorium, designed to seat 1200, can be isolated by means of movable panels from three cantilevered seating areas, each of which can in turn be transformed into separate, smaller auditoriums. From the exterior of the building, they appear as three oblique volumes projecting in different directions, as if they were literally popping out of the main volume of the building, creating an extraordinarily intense sculptural affect. This masterpiece of constructivism recently underwent restoration. Some of the elements which had been altered during the Soviet era were restored to their original condition.
With the exception of his competition entry for Zuev, awarded to Ilya Golosov, all of Melnikov's projects for workers' clubs, including Kauchuk, Frunze, Burevestnik, Svoboda and Pravda, were built, albeit with significant alterations with respect to the original projects. They are still visible today.

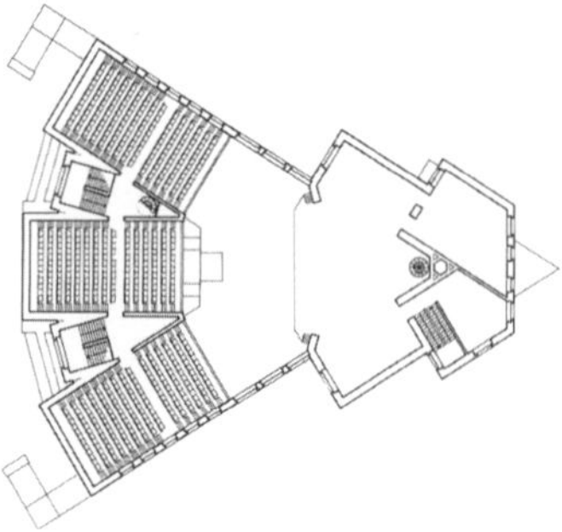

architects
K. Melnikov

type
cultural

construction
1927-1929

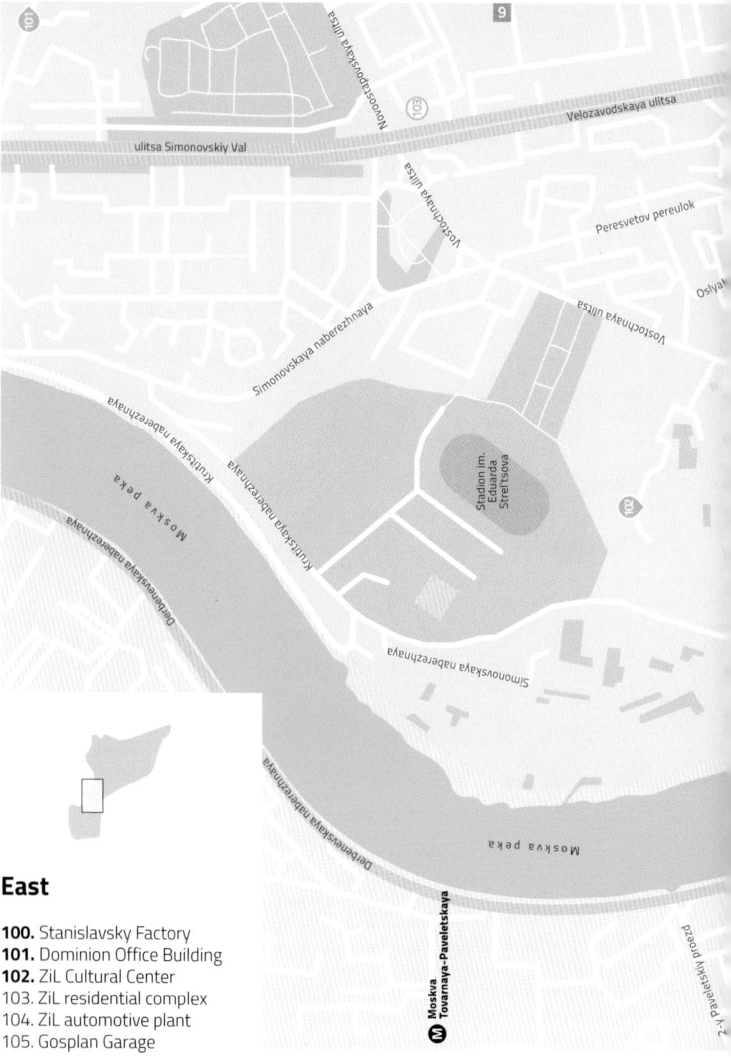

East

100. Stanislavsky Factory
101. Dominion Office Building
102. ZiL Cultural Center
103. ZiL residential complex
104. ZiL automotive plant
105. Gosplan Garage

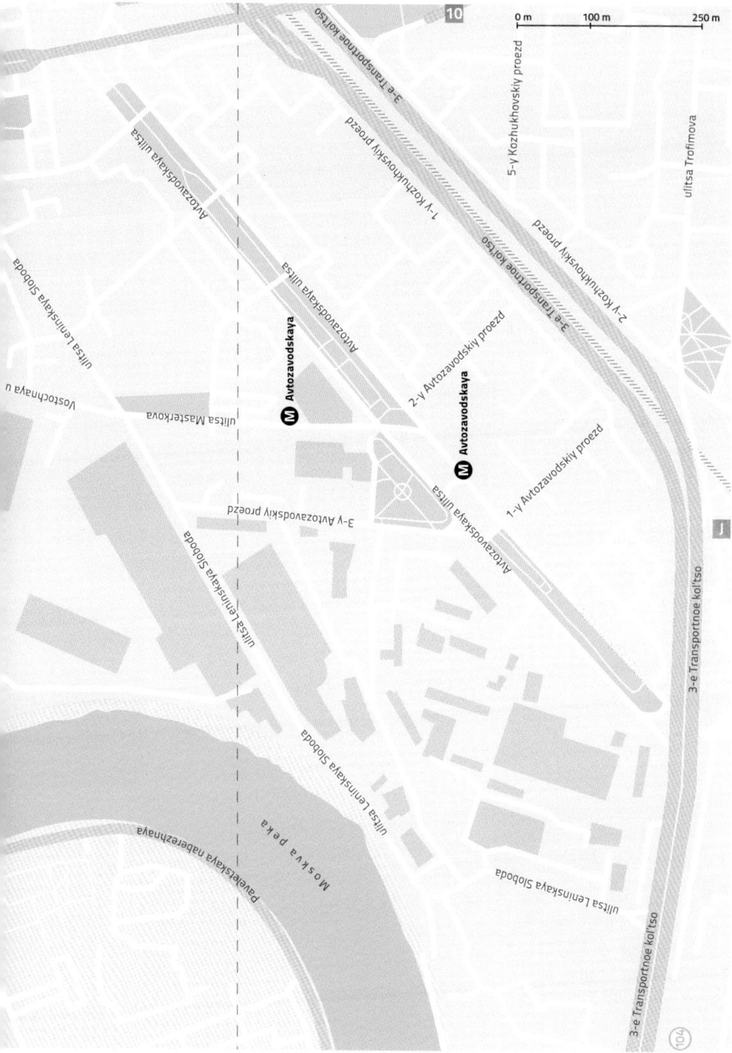
10
0 m
100 m
250 m
3-e Transportnoe kol'tso
5-y Kozhukhovskiy proezd
ulitsa Trofimova
1-y Kozhukhovskiy proezd
Avtozavodskaya ulitsa
2-y Kozhukhovskiy proezd
ulitsa Leninskaya Sloboda
Avtozavodskaya
2-y Avtozavodskiy proezd
Vostochnaya u
ulitsa Masterkova
Avtozavodskaya
1-y Avtozavodskiy proezd
3-y Avtozavodskiy proezd
J
M o s k v a p e k a
Paveletskaya naberezhnaya
104

100. Stanislavsky Factory

Stanislavskogo ulitsa 21c3
109004 Moscow

external viewing only

8 > Marksistskaya

53 > Aleksandra Solzhenitsyna ulitsa; **45/53** > Pestovsky pereulok - Teatr kukol

The first project completed in Moscow by the British firm John McAslan + Partners, the Stanislavsky Factory is a remarkable example of regeneration of an abandoned industrial area. The project has earned much praise for the sensitive manner in which it combines refurbished historic elements and new interventions, resulting in a highly successful functional program. For a considerable period it acted as a benchmark for the innovative adaptive re-use of historic buildings in Moscow.
Originally built by the Stanislavsky family, leading industrialists and cultural patrons of late-Imperial Russia, the complex includes a theater built by one of the family's most illustrious members, the renowned director Kostantin Stanislavsky. Today the former factory has been converted to mixed-use business and cultural activities. Thirteen buildings host offices, luxury apartments, a hotel, and a restaurant, over a total surface area of approximately 30,000 sq m.
Special attention was paid to the common areas and collective outdoor spaces, which feature refined urban landscaping and furnishing solutions.

© John McAslan + Partners

architects
John McAslan + Partners

type
commercial, cultural

construction
2006-2010

101. Dominion Office Building

Sharikopodshipnikovskaya ulitsa 5
115088 Moscow

external viewing only

20/40/43 > TsNIITMash

10 > Dubrovka

9 > Shinny zavod;
156/299/608 > Zheleznodorozhny pereezd

26 > Shinny zavod

The Dominion office complex is not far from the former site of the GPZ-1 ball-bearing factory, which was built in the early 1930s with the help of FIAT-RIV in Turin, Italy.
The structure was conceived as a series of superimposed platforms staggered at every level and linked by a series of curved catwalks crossing a full-height atrium in the middle.
The atrium provides a shared central space at the ground floor, with a restaurant and cafeteria, and natural light for the interior balconies from above.
The offices are hosted in standard, rectilinear volumes that offer tenants a range of floor areas. Situated around the edge of the atrium, the vertical circulation and service spaces act as a filter with respect to the offices, and, together with a row of columns around the perimeter, support the loads of the platforms.

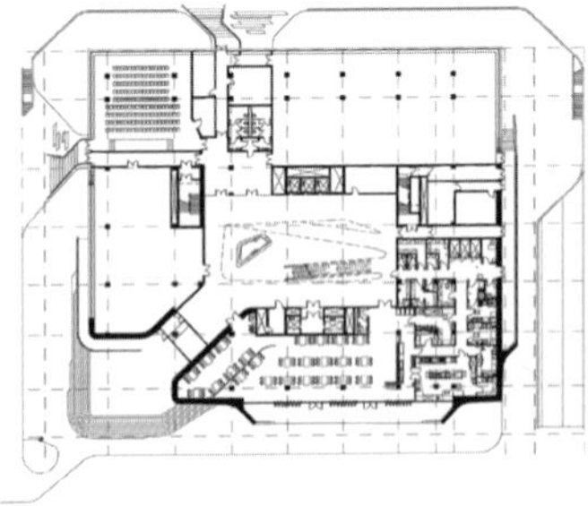

architects
Zaha Hadid Architects

type
offices

construction
2015

102. ZiL Cultural Center

Vostochnaya ulitsa 4
115280 Moscow

external viewing only

2 > Avtozavodskaya

8/9/99/186/193/950
> Zavod Dinamo

26/67 > Zavod Dinamo

The construction of centers for the recreation and education of workers led, in the 1930s, to the creation of a new building type: the Palace of Culture. One of the most famous of these "palaces" was designed by the Vesnin brothers for the ZiL autoplant workers union. The architects designed a complex articulated in three volumes: a theater building (never built) with a large 4000-seat auditorium, which was meant to function as the fulcrum of the entire composition, creating a precise spatial and volumetric hierarchy, the actual workers' club, which is cross-shaped in plan, and a small auditorium for 1200 people. The club and the small auditorium were built between 1933 and 1937. The project as a whole was never completed due to a radical shift in attitude against modernist architecture. Though the ZiL Palace underwent alterations during the post-war period, the appearance and original layout of the complex have remained substantially unchanged. Not far from the worker's club is the ZiL automotive plant, the most important in the country during the 1930s-1950s. The facade of the management building was Konstantin Melnikov's first professional commission, while the Vesnin brothers provided consultation for subsequent expansions of the industrial buildings. The huge factory complex, now largely in disuse and partially demolished, is presently undergoing a new phase of transformation based on a master plan by the firm Proekt Meganom.

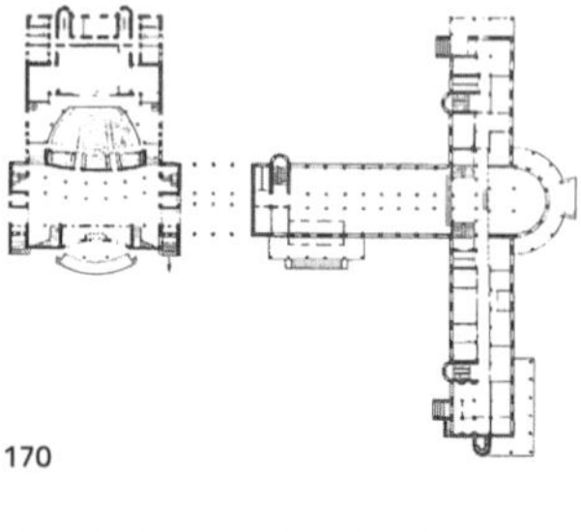

architects
L. Vesnin

type
cultural

construction
1931-1937

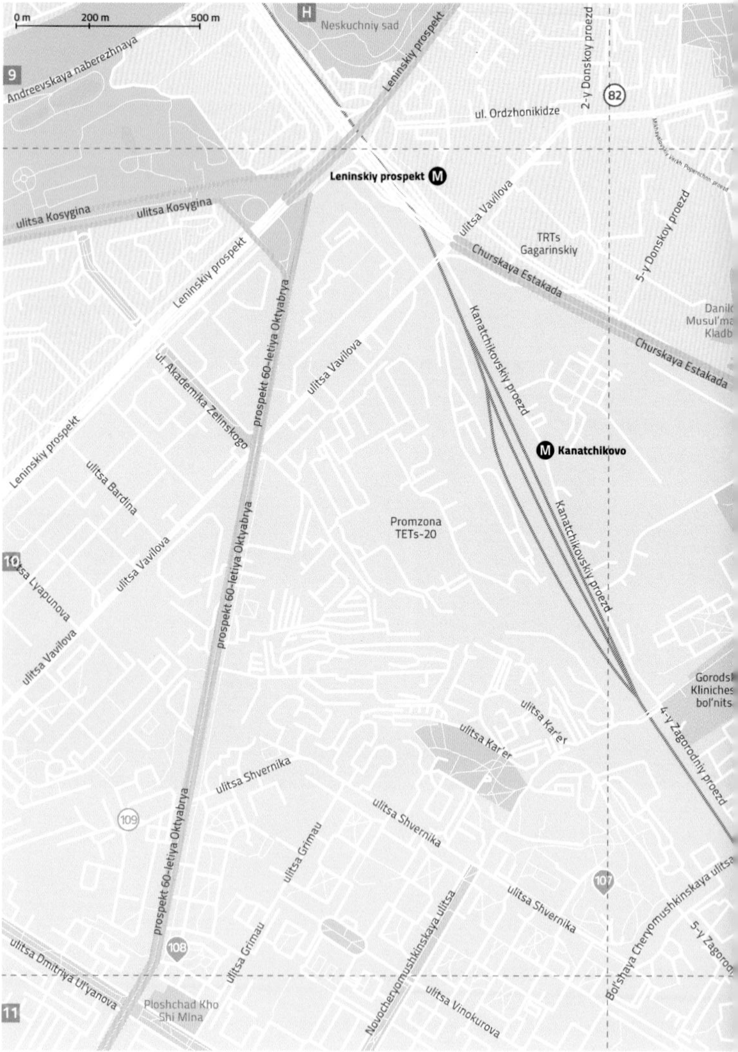
0 m
200 m
500 m
9
10
11
Neskuchniy sad
Andreevskaya naberezhnaya
Leninskiy prospekt
2-y Donskoy proezd
82
ul. Ordzhonikidze
Leninskiy prospekt
ulitsa Kosygina
ulitsa Kosygina
ulitsa Vavilova
TRTs
Gagarinskiy
Churskaya Estakada
5-y Donskoy proezd
Leninskiy prospekt
prospekt 60-letiya Oktyabrya
ulitsa Vavilova
Kanatchikovskiy proezd
Churskaya Estakada
ul. Akademika Zelinskogo
Leninskiy prospekt
Kanatchikovo
ulitsa Bardina
Promzona
TETs-20
Kanatchikovskiy proezd
ulitsa Vavilova
prospekt 60-letiya Oktyabrya
ulitsa Vavilova
4-y Zagorodniy proezd
ulitsa Kar'er
ulitsa Kar'er
ulitsa Shvernika
109
ulitsa Shvernika
prospekt 60-letiya Oktyabrya
ulitsa Grimau
107
ulitsa Shvernika
Novocheryomushkinskaya ulitsa
108
ulitsa Grimau
ulitsa Dmitriya Ul'yanova
Ploshchad Kho
Shi Mina
ulitsa Vinokurova
Bol'shaya Cheryomushkinskaya ulitsa

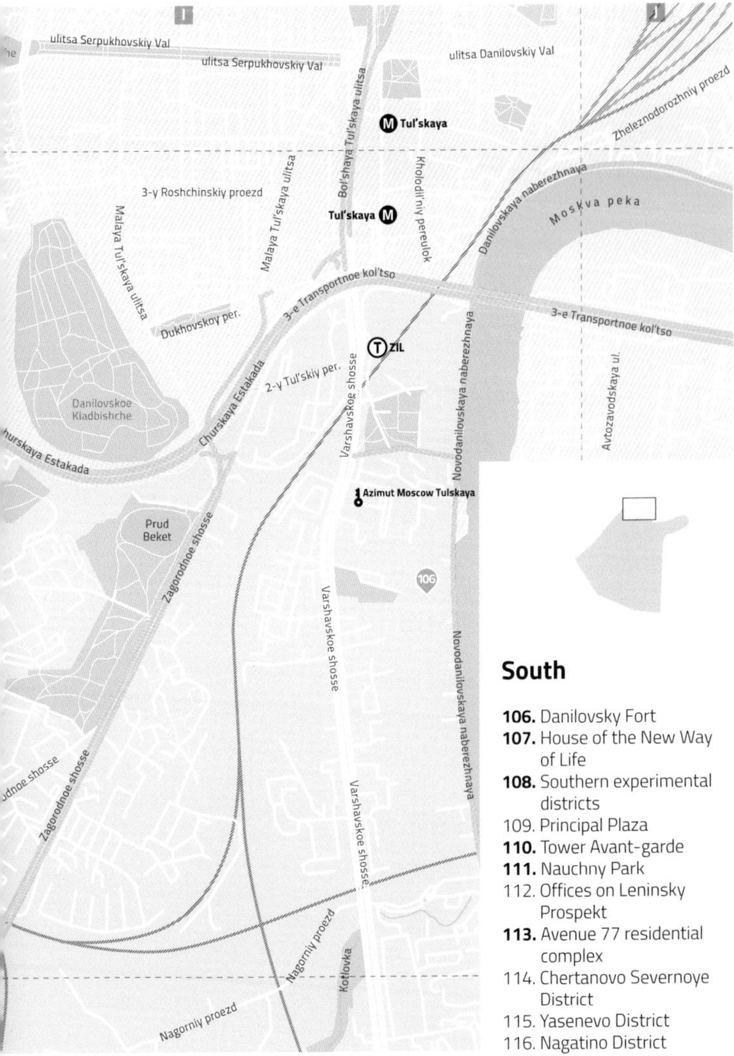

South

106. Danilovsky Fort
107. House of the New Way of Life
108. Southern experimental districts
109. Principal Plaza
110. Tower Avant-garde
111. Nauchny Park
112. Offices on Leninsky Prospekt
113. Avenue 77 residential complex
114. Chertanovo Severnoye District
115. Yasenevo District
116. Nagatino District

106. Danilovsky Fort

Novodanilovskaya naberezhnaya 10
117105 Moscow

external viewing only

3/16/35/47 >
Stadion Trud

9 > Tulskaya

ZiIL

25/44/142/147/ 275/700/907 >
Stadion Trud

1/1к/8/40/46/71 >
Stadion Trud

This business center overlooking the south bank of the Moskva River stands out from the general landscape of commercial buildings in contemporary Moscow, with its intricate play of volumes and the lively tones and textures of its brick cladding. It is one of the best works of architecture the city has seen in recent years.

The complex is formed by three autonomous vertical blocks of varying heights (6, 12, and 15 floors) and a shared, transparent ground-floor volume that unifies the complex and mediates its relationship with the land. The clarity and rationality of the layout are balanced by the complexity of the facades. The projecting volumes and the irregular size and arrangement of the openings give rhythm to the main facade, while graceful curves and indentations soften the edges of its forms.

The rooftop of the continuous ground-level volume features an open courtyard with a grassy hill at its center, punctuated by skylights.

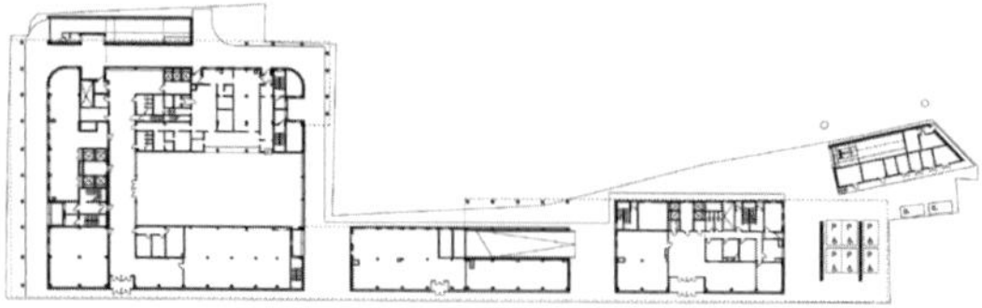

architects
Sergey Skuratov Architects

type
offices

construction
2005-2009

107. House of the New Way of Life

Shvernika ulitsa 19
117449 Moscow

external viewing only

26/38/38k > Shvernika ulitsa

6 > Akademicheskaya

41/121 > Shvernika ulitsa

The "Dom novogo byta" or DNB (House of the New Way of Life) bears witness to the experimental vein of 1960s Soviet architecture which was open to innovative and radical Western ideas and interested in rediscovering the protagonists and movements that had flourished during the revolutionary climate of the USSR during the 1920s. The complex was designed by a collective directed by Natan Osterman which drew inspiration from the communal apartment blocks of earlier times while employing modern technologies. It consists of two sixteen-story residential towers, positioned symmetrically. The wings of each tower are arranged in plan at an obtuse angle, so that the buildings resemble gigantic open books. A lower volume links the two towers and houses collective spaces for services and recreational activities. The main facades of the buildings are dominated by a succession of strip windows, while the ends feature structural grids that mark the rhythm of a series of loggias. The apartments are distributed in groups of 12 to 15 along an interior street -like corridor. They were furnished with only basic kitchenettes and were served by a cafeteria-style restaurant.

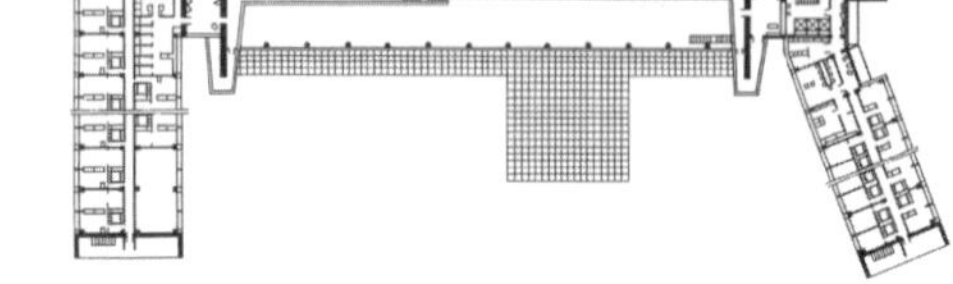

© Denis Esakov

architects
N. Osterman, A. Petrushkova

type
residential

construction
1969

108. Southern experimental districts

Prospekt 60 Letya Oktyabrya
117449 Moscow

external viewing only

6 > Akademicheskaya

67/67k/119/121/142 /196/218/218k/786 > Akademicheskaya

The "Plan Rekonstruktsii Moskvy," the 1935 General Plan for the reconstruction of Moscow, called for expansion of the metropolis towards the southwest, owing to the beauty and healthful qualities of the area. The plan was confirmed during the postwar period and began to be implemented in the early 1950s with the construction of the new residential complexes by Aleksandr Vlasov in the Yugo-Zapadny rayons (the south-west administrative districts), along the Leninsky prospekt starting from Gagarin Square. The "experimental" housing district of Novye Cheryomushki (plan) was built following the death of Stalin (1953) and Khrushchev's laments against monumentalism. "Open" planning arrangements, a complete absence of decorative elements, and housing blocks with "minimal" but single-family dwellings were all indications that a profound revolution had taken place in the approach to mass-produced housing. This was the origin of the "Khrushchyovka," the minimal five-story housing blocks that began to dot the suburbs of Moscow and other cities throughout the Soviet Union from the end of the 1950s. The residential experimentation in this area culminated between the 1970s and 1980s with the imposing megastructures of Troparyovo, Ivanovskoe, Chertanovo Severnoye (photo) and Nagatino.

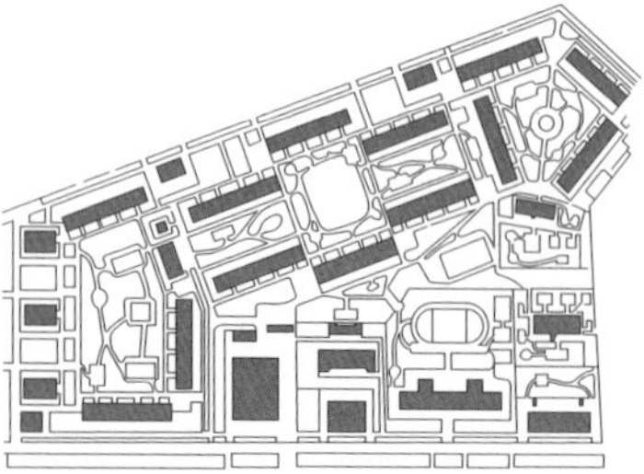

© Denis Esakov

architects
N. Osterman, S. Lyashchenko, G. Pavlov, V. Svirsky, V. Kalafatov, M. Fradin, J. Dichter, V. Nidelman

type
residential

construction
1956-1958

110. Avant-garde Tower

Novocheremushkinskaya ulitsa 60
117420 Moscow

external viewing only

6 > Novye Cheryomushki

103/113/246/684 >
Proyektiruemy proezd
№ 4668

The Avant-garde residential tower, with its unmistakable oval plan, is located at the intersection of ulitsa Novocheremishkinskaya and ulitsa Garibaldi. The urbanization of the surrounding suburban neighborhood was launched in the late 1950s by Novye Cheryomushki's historic project for a model district. A stratification of residential projects from successive periods provides an illustration of the various cycles that have characterized mass housing in the late Soviet and post-Soviet eras.
In this context of large monochrome housing blocks, it is easy to understand the architect's decision to clad the new residential tower with brightly colored materials, making the building stand out as a vibrant new landmark in the neighborhood.

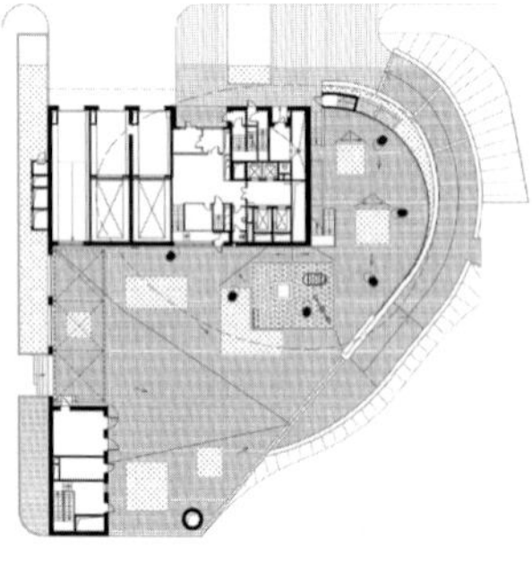

© Sergey Kisselev

architects	**type**	**construction**
S. Kisselev	residential	2004-2006

111. Nauchny Park

Nauchny proezd 14A
117246 Moscow

external viewing only

6 > Kaluzhskaya

246 > Khersonskaya ulitsa dom 32;
1/28/41/163/224/246/258/624/671/699/784 > Ulitsa Vvedenskogo

The project commissioned to the firm ADM for the design of this business park called for the renovation of a building complex erected around 1970 in the Soviet style.
Superimposed over the regular sequence of openings of the existing facades is an exterior skin, articulated in wood panels, colored fiber-cement panels and glass panels, arranged rhythmically along metal runners at the height of the windowsills. This arrangement emphasizes the independent nature of this second building envelope and its function as a screen.
The upright wood panels are positioned in both the sailor and soldier positions, creating shadows that give the facade depth and variety.
Terraces at the top levels of the buildings feature wood decking and parapets.
The business park occupies a 2 hectare area surrounded by parkland. In summertime, the green vegetation dominates visually, and the boundary between the buildings and nature begins to fade.
And important characteristic of the project is the careful design of the exterior spaces, including walkways, furnishings, signage, and lighting.

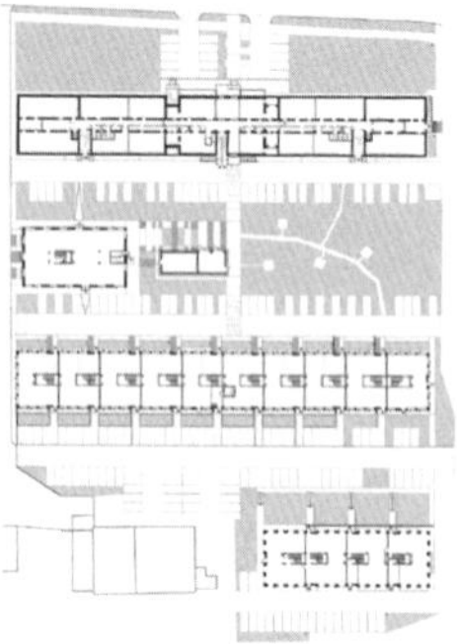

© ADM

© ADM

architects
ADM

type
offices

construction
2011-2013

113. Avenue 77 residential complex

Chertanovo Severnoye mkr 1A
117648 Moscow

external viewing only

1/16 > Tsentr tvorchestva

9 > Chertanovskaya

168/624 > Tsentr tvorchestva

The Avenue 77 residential complex is composed of three high-rise volumes, each with 40 floors and two underground levels which, together with the adjacent 24-story buildings, form a sort of enclosed courtyard. An eight-story office block stands to one side. The main entrance to the high-rise residential towers is from the west, by means of a ramp. Panoramic lifts are located on both the east side of the complex, near the Chertanovskaya metro station, and on the west side. They are open to the public and lead from the ground-floor level directly to the top of their respective towers. Access to the various functional areas is differentiated by the considerable variation in ground levels. The main entrance to the shopping mall and entertainment center, located on the east side, is linked directly to the pedestrian zone between the metro station and the Novye Chertanovo residential district.

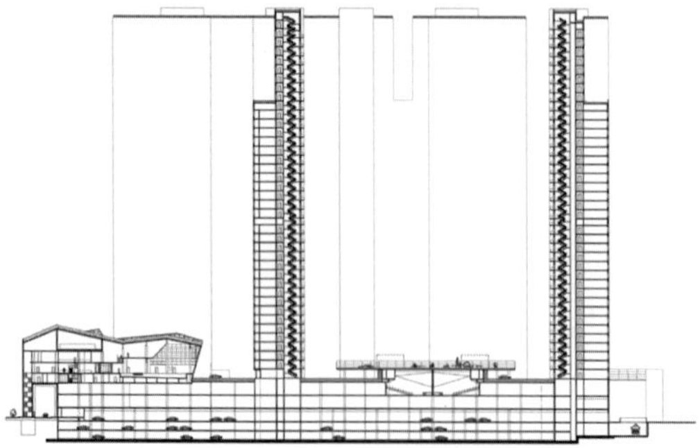

© Reserve

architects
Reserve

type
residential

construction
2005-2009

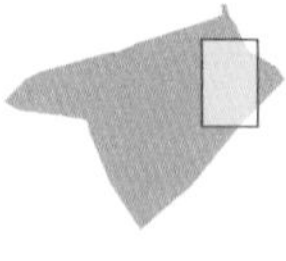

West

117. Mosfilmovsky
118. Moscow State University
119. Luzhniki Stadium
120. Young Pioneers Palace
121. Yugo-Zapadny District
122. Troparyovo District
123. Skolkovo Moscow School of Management
124. Matrex
125. Hypercube
126. Mercury Theater
127. Luxury Village
128. Barvikha Hotel

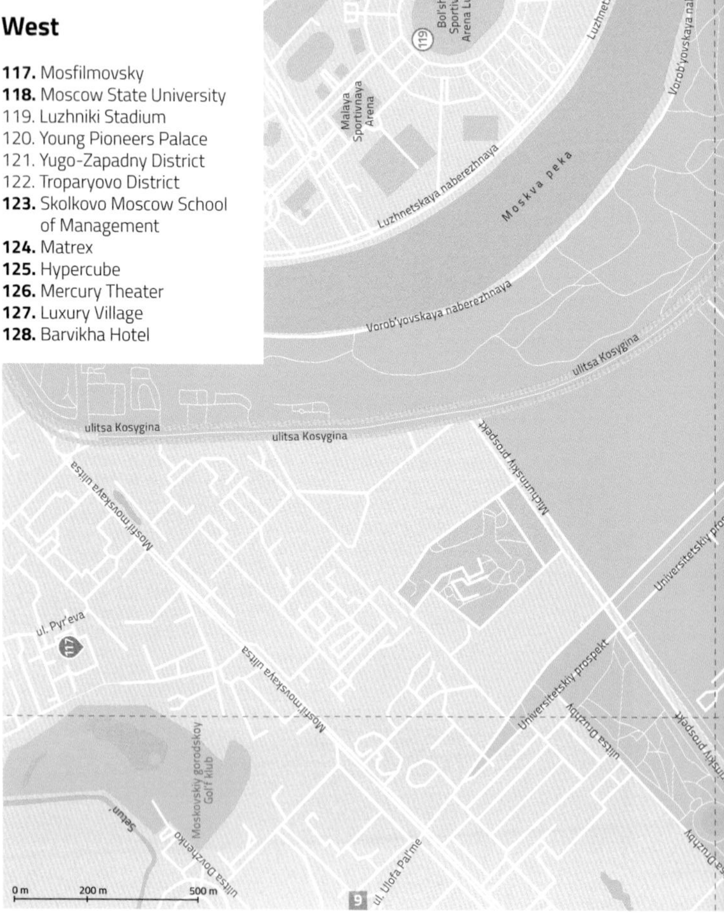

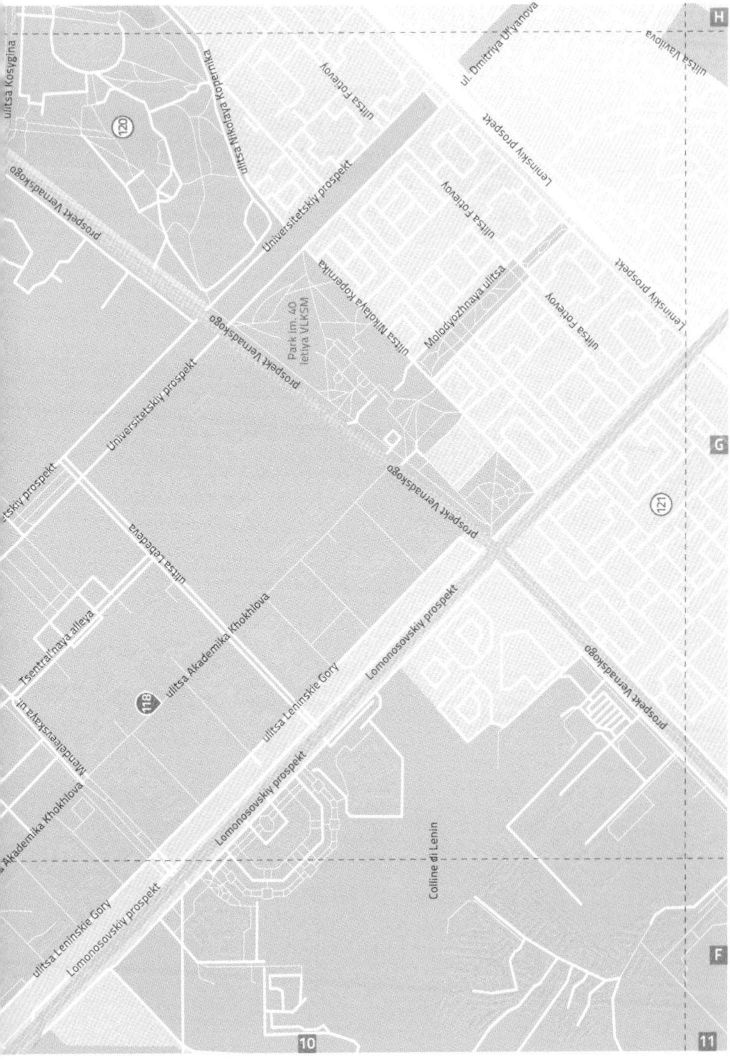
H
G
F
10
11
ulitsa Kosygina
120
ulitsa Nikolaya Kopernika
ulitsa Fotievoy
ul. Dmitriya Ul'yanova
ulitsa Vavilova
Leninskiy prospekt
prospekt Vernadskogo
Universitetskiy prospekt
ulitsa Fotievoy
Park im. 40 letiya VLKSM
ulitsa Nikolaya Kopernika
Molodyozhnaya ulitsa
Leninskiy prospekt
ulitsa Fotievoy
prospekt Vernadskogo
Universitetskiy prospekt
prospekt Vernadskogo
121
ulitsa Lebedeva
Tsentral'naya alleya
ulitsa Akademika Khokhlova
118
Lomonosovskiy prospekt
ulitsa Leninskie Gory
prospekt Vernadskogo
Mendeleevskaya ul.
Akademika Khokhlova
Lomonosovskiy prospekt
Colline di Lenin
ulitsa Leninskie Gory
Lomonosovskiy prospekt

117. Mosfilmovsky

Pyryeva ulitsa 5
119285 Moscow

external viewing only

3/8 > Park Pobedy

119/205/205к > Mosfilm

17/34/34к > Mosfilm

This apartment complex on ulitsa Pyryeva was the first "deluxe" skyscraper in Moscow. The underlying idea was to return architecture to its sculptural grandeur. The complex consists of two towers united by a simple low-rise structure. The taller tower features a complex pattern of windows that increase in size as the floors progress upwards. The sequence of changes is accentuated by four types of colored panels, from dark gray at the ground level and progressively becoming brilliant white at the upper floors. The facade of the shorter tower is clad with a combination of aluminum modules and frosted glass panels, in three different degrees of opacity, which conceal the window openings and masonry surfaces. The glass panels are tilted in different directions so that they reflect both land and sky. The design and materials of the interiors are on par with the standards of a five-star hotel. The complex also houses large shopping and entertainment areas, restaurants and a supermarket.

© Sergey Skuratov Architects

architects
Sergey Skuratov Architects

type
residential, commercial

construction
2006-2008

118. Moscow State University

Leninskye Gory ulitsa 1
119991 Moscow

open to public

+7 (045) 9391000

www.msu.ru

14/22/26/39 > Universitet

1 > Universitet

47/67/103/130/130к/187/260 > Biblioteka MGU;
57/119/661/Б/н > DK MGU;
1/113 > Ulitsa Lebedeva;
1/57/111/113/119/661/715 > Mendeleevskaya ulitsa
A > Tsirk

34/34к > Biblioteka MGU;
7 > Universitetskaya ploshchad;
28 > Tsirk

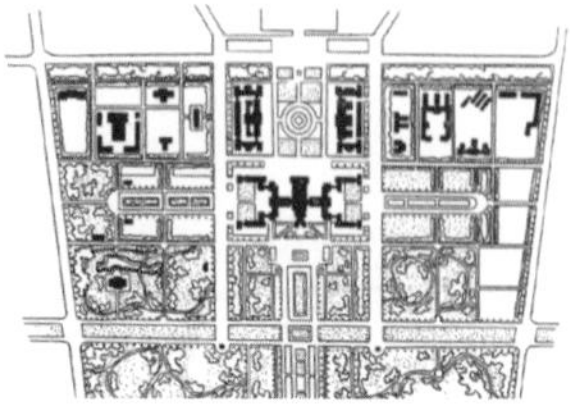

The Stalinist program of high-rise buildings (Stalinskie Vysotki) found its best expression in the series of seven skyscrapers erected in Moscow between 1948 and 1953. They remain centered around the never-built Palace of the Soviets, which explains their positioning in strategic locations throughout the city, where they mark important nodes in the urban landscape. The most famous and impressive of the group is the main building of Moscow State University (MGU). Situated on Sparrow Hills, formerly Lenin Hills, it overlooks the principal axis of expansion of the city in the southwest direction. This "Citadel of Culture," the program for which included the surrounding landscaping, was built between 1949 and 1953 to a design by a collective of famous architects of the period (Lev Rudnev, Sergej Chernyschev, and Pavel Abrosimov).

The other Vysotki are:
the Ministry of Foreign Affairs building (Vladimir Gelfreykh, Mikhail Minkus) / the Red Gate Building, which formerly housed the Ministry of Transport (Alexey Dushkin, Boris Mezencev, Viktor Abramov) / Hotel Leningradskaya (Leonid Polyakov, Andrey Boretskiy) / Hotel Ukraina (Arkady Mordvinov, Vyacheslav Oltarzhevsky, Pavel Krasilnikov) / the Kotelnicheskaya Embankment building (Dmitri Chechulin, Andrei Rostkovsky) / the Kudrinskaya Square residential building (Mikhail Posokhin, Ashot Mndoyants, M. N. Vokhomsky).

architects
L. Rudnev, S. Chernyshev

type
educational

construction
1949-1953

123. Skolkovo Moscow School of Management

Novaya ulitsa 100 Skolkovo village Odintsovsky district
143025 Moscow

external viewing only

+7 (495) 5393003
info@skolkovo.ru
www.skolkovo.ru

205/205з/818/818к/ 867 > Povorot na sovkhoz Zarechye

The design of the Skolkovo Moscow School of Management was based on the promotion of an innovative approach to education in a large, self-contained structure. Due to its remote location and in consideration of the cold Moscow winters, the structure was conceived as an independent, multifunctional building. The main elements of the school are in fact contained in a single building that provides access to a series of services without needing to exit the structure.
The housing units are designed to accommodate students, teachers, and administrative staff, as well as guests attending conferences or short courses.
The core of the building, circular in form, comprises the teaching spaces, a conference center and academic support facilities, all of which face onto an interior courtyard. Additional box-shaped volumes jut out from the roof of the main structure, containing a well-being center, administrative offices, and the residential blocks.

© Adjaye Associates

architects
Adjaye Associates

type
educational

construction
2010

124. Matrex

Ulitsa Bleza Paskalya
143025 Moscow

open to public

Tryokhgorka

Matrex is a hybrid structure designed to accommodate multiple functions, including apartments, innovative work spaces, a multipurpose hall, exhibition spaces, and a restaurant-café. Original and unique, it embodies the most innovative aspects of architecture, art and technology, including advanced approaches to ergonomics and sustainability.
The building takes the form of a transparent truncated pyramid delineated by a structural grid in reinforced concrete. Its central core is completely occupied by a full-height atrium in the unmistakable shape of a gigantic matryoshka doll, making for a spectacular sight when the lights go on after dark.
Both the vertical transport systems — panoramic stairs and elevators — and the functional spaces at each of the floors are positioned around the perimeter of the building. The base of the matryoshka-shaped atrium can be configured in a variety of ways. A ramp spirals up around the atrium to the top of the building. The walls along the ramp serve as exhibition space and are equipped with a special system for rotating the works on view.

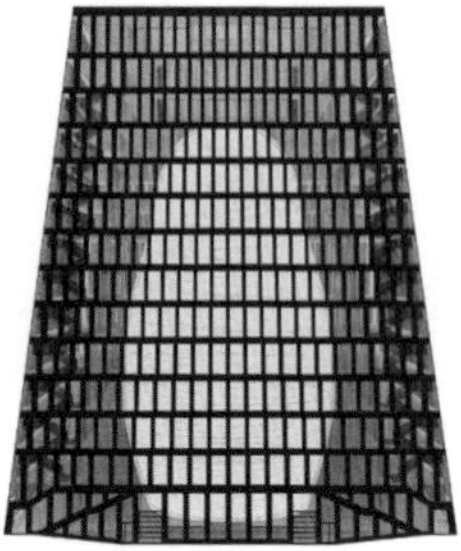

architects	**type**	**construction**
Bernaskoni Architectural Bureau	multipurpose	2012-2015

125. Hypercube

Ulitsa Malevicha 1
143025 Moscow

external viewing only

Tryokhgorka

Hypercube was the first building to be erected as part of the ambitious plan for the Skolkovo Innovation Center, a scientific and technological research hub.
This highly experimental and groundbreaking edifice by Boris Bernaskoni is capable of adapting itself over time to a wide range of possible requirements.
The structural system consists of a framework of columns around the perimeter, with the service blocks positioned on opposite sides, leaving the central core of the building and the two remaining sides completely free of hindrance.
The architect, who compares his project to the International Space Station, comments "Hypercube is a physical zone of innovation and experimentation in the fields of architecture, engineering, art, and media."

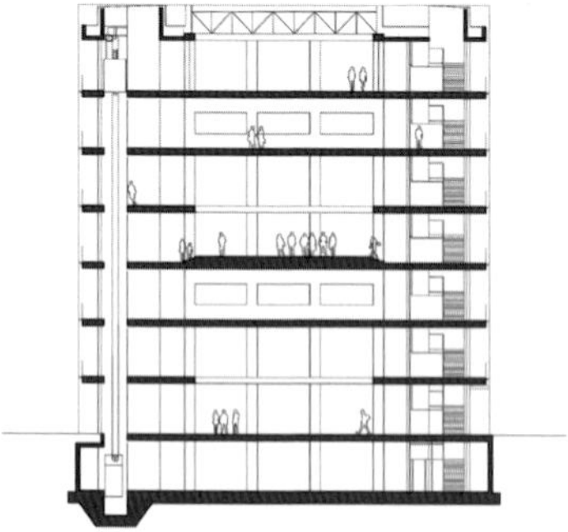

© Bernaskoni Architectural Bureau

architects
Bernaskoni Architectural Bureau

type
multipurpose

construction
2011-2013

126. Mercury Theater

Rublevo-Uspenskoye shosse 114
143083 Moscow

by appointment

+7 (495) 9333399

www.barvikhaconcerthall.ru

Barvikha

The fluidity of form of the Mercury Theater marks one end of the Luxury Village shopping mall, with the foyer interior forming a continuous space with the public square in front of the building.
A series of vertical, wave-shaped blades creates a deep facade whose a dynamic effect is perceived from both the exterior of the buildings and from within the foyer.
The central auditorium, the interiors of which were designed by the architect Antonio Citterio, is a flexible environment that can be used as a theater or for fashion shows or other types of events. The various floor sections can be arranged in a variety of geometrical configurations with the aid of eight hydraulic mechanisms.
When configured as a theater, the space can host up to 600 spectators in the stalls and 50 people in the two tiers of box seats.

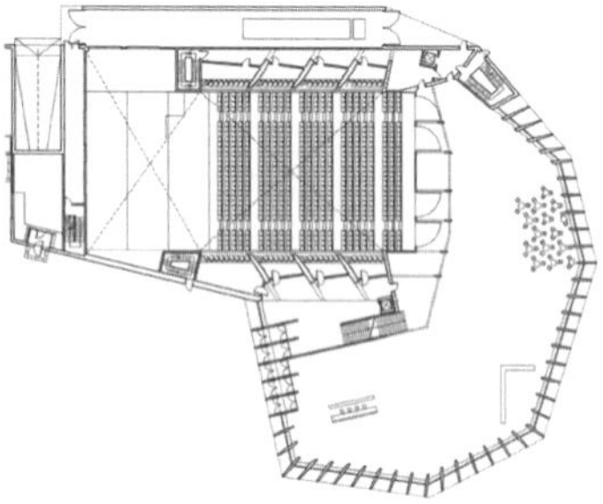

architects
Proekt Meganom

type
cultural

construction
2003-2006

127. Luxury Village

Rublevo-Uspenskoye shosse 114c8
143083 Moscow

January - December
Mon - Sun / 10 am - 10 pm

+7 (495) 9806804

www.blv.ru

Barvikha

The Luxury Village shopping complex creates a sort of instant fragment of urban fabric in Barvikha, an elite rural zone east of Moscow that was already a privileged location during the Soviet era. The main axis of the complex acts as a pedestrian promenade with a sequence of five squares, a theater at one end, and a hotel at the other. Along each side of this public walkway is an elegant series of buildings in red cedar and glass that showcase the world's most prestigious luxury brands.
The refined architecture of this high-end modern development contrasts sharply with the historic eclecticism that so often characterizes similar operations that were undertaken in Moscow in the 1990s.

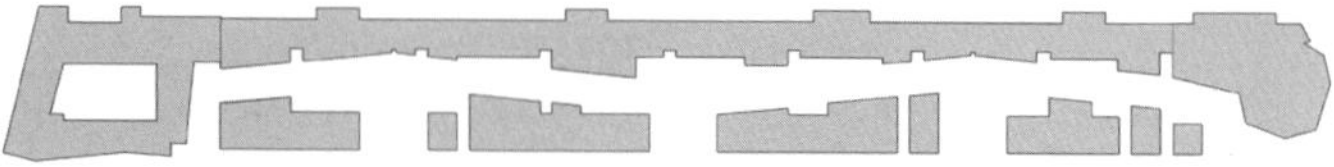

architects
Proekt Meganom

type
commercial

construction
2003-2006

128. Barvikha Hotel

Rublevo-Uspenskoye shosse 114c3
143083 Moscow

external viewing only

+7 (495) 2258880
info@barvikhahotel.com
www.barvikhahotel.com

Barvikha

Designed by Antonio Citterio, one of the world's leading architects, the Barvikka Hotel & Spa is an extremely modern structure that responds perfectly to the requirements of superior quality and refined brand recognition imposed by the exclusive context of the entire Luxury Village.
The guiding idea of the project was to create stylish environments with pleasant views while at the same time protecting the privacy of guests. The articulated building volumes are arranged around a green interior courtyard, the facades of which are clad with a series of attractive vertical wooden slats. The guestrooms average 65 sq m in size and feature private terraces, discreetly screened by the wood cladding of the facade. The entrance to the building, consisting of a winter garden surrounded by green glazing, opens onto a refined and welcoming lobby centered on a large fireplace. A 1200 sq m space in the partially below ground level hosts sophisticated spa facilities and an indoor swimming pool.

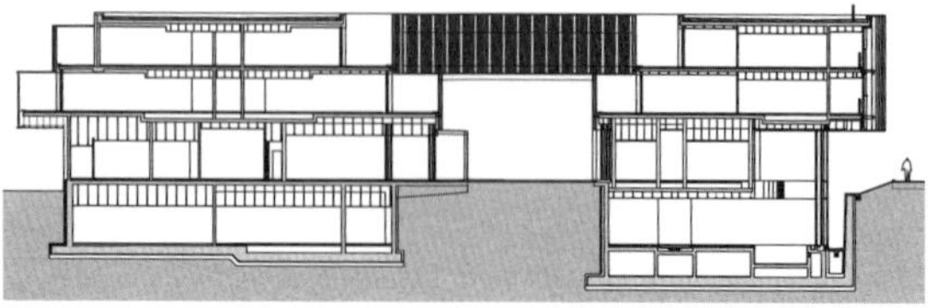

architects
Antonio Citterio Patricia Viel and Partners

type
hotel

construction
2009

Museums and Exhibition Centers

Pushkin State Museum of Fine Arts
Museum of fine arts
-
Volkhonka ulitsa 12, 121019 Moscow

www.arts-museum.ru

Tel +7 (495) 6979578

New Tretayakov Gallery
Gallery of Russian avant-garde
-
Krymsky Val ulitsa 10, 119017 Moscow

www.tretyakovgallery.ru
tretyakov@tretyakov.ru
Tel +7 (499) 2381378

Schusev State Museum of Architecture
Museum of architecture
-
Vozdvizhenka ulitsa 5/25, 119019 Moscow

www.muar.ru
schusevmuseum@gmail.com
Tel +7 (495) 6973874

Tretyakov Gallery
Museum of Russian art
-
Lavrushkinsky pereulok 10, 119017 Moscow

www.tretyakovgallery.ru
tretyakov@tretyakov.ru
Tel +7 (495) 9511362

Moscow Kremlin Museums
Historical and cultural museum
-
Krasnaya ploshchad, 103073 Moscow

www.kreml.ru

Tel +7 (495) 6953776

MAMM – Multimedia Art Museum, Moscow
Multimedia art museum
-
Ostozhenka ulitsa 16, 119034 Moscow

www.mamm-mdf.ru
info@mdf.ru
Tel +7 (495) 6371100

Winzavod
Center for contemporary art
-
Syromyatnicheskaya naberezhnaya 1, 105120 Moscow

www.winzavod.ru
winzavod@winzavod.ru
Tel +7 (495) 9174646

Garage
Museum of contemporary art
-
Krymsky Val ulitsa 9, Gorky Park, 119049 Moscow

www.garageccc.com
welcome@garageccc.com
Tel +7 (495) 6450520

Krasny Oktyabr
Temporary exhibition space
-
Bersenevskaya nabereznaya 6, 119072 Moscow

www.paintart.ru

Tel +7 (495) 2300733

Moscow Manege
Temporary exhibition hall
-
Manezhnaya ploshchad 1,109012
Moscow

www.moscowmanege.ru
info@moscowmanege.ru
Tel +7 (495) 6459277

New Manege
Temporary exhibition hall
-
Georgiyevsky pereulok 3c3,
125009 Moscow

www.new-manege.ru

Ema
Temporary exhibition space
-
Bolshoy Nikolovorobinskiy pereulok 7c8,
109028 Moscow

Tel +7 (495) 2253087

Artplay
Center for architecture and design
-
Nizhnyaya Syromyatnicheskaya ulitsa 10,
105120 Moscow

www.artplay.ru

Tel +7 (495) 6200883

Flacon Design Factory
Design center
-
Bolshaya Novodmitrovskaya ulitsa 36,
127015 Moscow

www.flacon.ru
info@flacon.ru
Tel +7 (495) 7907901

Yakut Galeriya – Arma – Gazgolder
Art gallery
-
Nizhny Susalny pereulok 5,
105064 Moscow

yakutgallery@gmail.ru
Tel +7 (495) 3145925

Art House
Temporary exhibition space
-
Serebryanicheskaya nabereznaya 19,
109028 Moscow

Tel +7 (495) 2682308

Theatres

Bolshoi Theatre
-
Teatralnaya ploshchad 1, 125009 Moscow

www.bolshoi.ru
Tel +7 (495) 4555555

MKhAT – Moscow Arts Theatre
-
Kamergersky pereulok 3, 125009 Moscow

www.mxat.ru
mxat@theatre.ru
Tel +7 (495) 6298760

Taganka Theatre
-
Zemlyanoy Val ulitsa 76/21, 109240 Moscow

www.taganka.theatre.ru
taganka@theatre.ru
Tel +7 (495) 9151217

Moscow State Conservatory P. I. Tchaikovsky
-
Bolshaya Nikitskaya ulitsa 13/6, 125009 Moscow

www.mosconsv.ru
spravka@mosconsv.ru
Tel +7 (495) 6299401

Moscow Operetta Theatre
-
Bolshaya Dmitrovka ulitsa 6, 125009 Moscow

www.mosoperetta.ru
Tel +7 (495) 9255050

Union of Composers
-
Bryusov pereulok 8/10c2, 125009 Moscow

www.house-composers.ru
allasedova2003@yandex.ru
Tel +7 (495) 6291365

Moscow International House of Music
-
Kosmodamianskaya nabereznaya 52 c8, 115035 Moscow

www.mmdm.ru
support@mmdm.ru
Tel +7 (495) 7301011

Arma Music Hall
-
Nizhny Susalny pereulok 5, стр. 5a, 105064 Moscow

www.ponominalu.ru
Tel +7 (495) 7876939

Illusion Cinema
-
Kotelnicheskaya nabereznaya 1/15, 109240 Moscow

www.illuzion-cinema.ru
Tel +7 (495) 9154353

Pioner Cinema
-
Kutuzovsky prospekt 21, 121151 Moscow

www.pioner-cinema.ru
Tel +7 (495) 2405240

Schools of Art and Architecture

Strelka Institute
-
Bersenevskaya nabereznaya 5,
119072 Moscow

www.strelka.com
more@strelka.com
Tel +7 (495) 2680619

MArchI – Moscow Architectural Institute
-
Rozhdestvenka ulitsa 11,
107031 Moscow

www.marhi.ru
office@markhi.ru
Tel +7 (495) 6234312

MARCH – The Moscow School of Architecture
-
Nizhnyaya Syromyatnicheskaya
ulitsa 10-5, 105120 Moscow

www.march.ru

Tel +7 (495) 6408015

Bookstores

Moskva
-
Tverskaya ulitsa 8, 125009 Moscow

www.moscowbooks.ru

Tel +7 (495) 2122208

Dom Knigi
-
Novy Arbat ulitsa 8, 121069 Moscow

www.mdk-arbat.ru

Tel +7 (499) 4004103

Falanster
-
Maly Gnezdnikovsky pereulok 12-27,
125009 Moscow

www.falanster.su

Tel +7 (495) 7495721

Biblio-Globus
-
Myasnitskaya ulitsa 6-3, 101000 Moscow

www.biblio-globus.ru
mail@biblio-globus.ru
Tel +7 (495) 7811925

Department Stores

TSUM Department Store
-
Petrovka ulitsa 2, 107031 Moscow

www.tsum.ru
hotline@tsum.ru
Tel +7 (495) 9337300

GUM Department Store
-
Krasnaya ploshchad 3, 101000 Moscow

www.gum.ru
info@gum.ru
Tel +7 (495) 7884343

Tsvetnoy
-
Tsvetnoy Bulvar 15, 127051 Moscow

www.tsvetnoy.com
info@tsvetnoy.com
Tel +7 (495) 7377773

Restaurants

Barashka
• • •
Petrovka ulitsa 20-1, 127051 Moscow

www.novikovgroup.ru
Tel +7 (495) 6252892

Pushkin
• • •
Tverskoy Bulvar 26a, 125009 Moscow

www.cafe-pushkin.ru
Tel +7 (495) 7390033

Dr. Zivago
• •
Mokhovaya ulitsa 15-1, 125009 Moscow

www.national.ru
Tel +7 (499) 9220100

Nedalniy Vostok
• •
Tverskoy Bulvar 15-2, 123104 Moscow

www.novikovgroup.ru
pr@novikovgroup.ru
Tel +7 (495) 6940154

Coffeemania
• •
Bolshaya Nikitskaya ulitsa 13-6 c1,
125009 Moscow

www.coffeemania.ru
Tel +7 (495) 7755188

Ragout
• •
Olimpiisky prospekt 16, 129090 Moscow

www.ragout.ru
cafe2@ragout.ru
Tel +7 (495) 7830461

Khachapuri
• •
Bolshoy Gnezdnikovsky pereulok 10, 103009 Moscow
www.hacha.ru
Tel +8 (985) 7643118

Jean-Jacques
• •
Nikitsky Bulvar 12, 119019 Moscow
www.jan-jak.com
info@tabletalk.ru
Tel +7 (495) 6903886

John Donne
• •
Nikitsky Bulvar 12, 119019 Moscow
www.john-donne.ru
Tel +7 (495) 6276907

Bar Cervetti
• •
Nikitsky Bulvar 8a, 119019 Moscow
www.barcervetti.ru
Tel +7 (495) 6492311

Strelka
• •
Bersenevskaya nabereznaya 14, 119072 Moscow
www.strelka.com
info@barstrelka.com
Tel +7 (495) 7717416

Lyudi kak lyudi
• •
Solyansky tupik 1-4, 107078 Moscow
www.ludikakludi.com
Tel +7 (495) 6211201

Ugolek
• •
Bolshaya Nikitskaya ulitsa 12 c1, 125009 Moscow
Tel +7 (495) 6290211

Denis Simachev Bar
• •
Stoleshnikov pereulok 12, 125009 Moscow
www.denissimachev.blogspot.it
Tel +7 (495) 6295702

Mayak
• •
Bolshaya Nikitskaya ulitsa 19, 121069 Moscow
www.clubmayak.ru
Tel +7 (495) 6917449

Door 19
• •
Serebryanicheskaya nabereznaya 19, 109028 Moscow
www.door19.ru
Tel +7 (499) 2682308

Stolovaya n. 57
•
Krasnaya ploshchad 3, 101000 Moscow
www.gum.ru
info@gum.ru
Tel +7 (495) 7884343

• • • expensive
• • mid-range
• inexpensive

Hotels

Hotel Metropol
• • •
Teatralniy proezd 2, 109012 Moscow
www.metropol-moscow.ru
metropol@metmos.ru
Tel +7 (499) 5017800

Hotel National
• • •
Mokhovaya ulitsa 15, 125009 Moscow
www.national.ru
Tel +7 (495) 2587000

Hotel Ukraina / Radisson Royal Hotel
• • •
Kutuzovsky prospekt 2, 121248 Moscow
www.radisson.ru
info.royal.moscow@radisson-hotels.ru
Tel +7 (495) 2215555

Hotel Hilton Moscow Leningradskaya
• • •
Kalanchevskaya ulitsa 21-40,
107078 Moscow
www.placeshilton.com/moscow

Hotel Pekin
• • •
Bolshaya Sadovaya ulitsa 5,
123001 Moscow
www.hotelpeking.ru
reservation@hotelpeking.ru
Tel +8 (800) 2500550

Hotel Best Holiday Inn
• •
Lesnaya ulitsa 15, 125047 Moscow
www.ihg.com
reservations@hi-mole.ru
Tel +7 (812) 3038647

Suschevsky Val ulitsa 74, 129272
Moscow
www.moscow-hi.ru
reservations@hi-mosu.ru
Tel +7 (495) 2258282

3 City Comfort Hotel
• •
Zlatoustinsky pereulok 3,
101000 Moscow
www.city-comfort.ru
citycomforthotels@mail.ru
Tel +7 (495) 2298018

Azimut Moscow Tulskaya
• •
Varshavskoe shosse 9, 117105 Moscow
www.azimuthotels.com
moscow@azimuthotels.com
Tel +8 (800) 2000048

Crossroads Hotel
• •
Kosmodamyanskaya naberezhnaya
32-34, 115035 Moscow
www.crossroads-hotels.ru
crossroads-hotels@yandex.ru
Tel +8 (800) 5557758

Ibis Moscow
• •
Shchipok ulitsa 22-1, 115184 Moscow
www.ibis.com
H7140@ACCOR.COM
Tel +7 (495) 6607500

Bakhrushina ulitsa 11, 115184 Moscow
www.ibis.com
H8223@ACCOR.COM
Tel +7 (495) 7205301

People Hotel
• •
Novinsky Bulvar 11, 121099 Moscow

www.en.hotel-people.ru
manager@hotel-people.ru
Tel +7 (495) 3634580

• • • expensive
• • mid-range
• inexpensive

Mini Hotel Chistoprudny
•
Chaplygina ulitsa 6, 101000 Moscow

www.1arbat-hotel.ru
booking@1arbat-hotel.ru
Tel + 7 (499) 2722042

Architectural offices

A. A. Chernikhov Design and Architecture Studio
-
Tsvetnoy Bulvar 30 c1, 127051 Moscow

chernikhovstudio.com
chernikhov@chernikhovstudio.com
Tel +7 (495) 7480243

ABD architects
-
Nizhny Susalny pereulok 5 c19, 105064 Moscow

www.abdcom.ru
amalyshev@abdcom.ru
Tel +7 (495) 9377686

ABV Group
-
Filippovsky pereulok 8 c1, 119019 Moscow

www.abv-group.ru
info@abv-group.ru
Tel +7 (495) 9252812

ADM Architects
-
Sushchevskaya ulitsa 27 c2, 127030 Moscow

adm-arch.ru
adm@adm-arch.ru
Tel +7 (495) 6650371

Alexander Brodsky
-
Bolshaya Sadovaya ulitsa 3 c7, 125047 Moscow

www.brod.it
gde-to@brod.it
Tel +7 (495) 2900402

Alexey Bavykin
-

www.bavykin.ru
info@bavykin.ru
Tel +7 (499) 2505106

Architectural Bureau Ostozhenka
-
Turchaninov pereulok 6 c2, 119034 Moscow

ostarch.ru
ostarch@ostarch.ru
Tel +7 (495) 7274224

Asadov Architectural Studio
-
Vavilova ulitsa 97, 117335 Moscow

www.asadov.ru
info@asadov.ru
Tel +7 (495) 9366650

Bernaskoni
-
Granatny pereulok 9, 123001 Moscow

bernaskoni.com
info@bernaskoni.com
Tel +7 (495) 6978379

Ilya Utkin
-
Pokrovka ulitsa, 28c1, 105064 Moscow

www.ilyautkin.ru
ilyautkin28@gmail.com

Mikhail Belov
-

arhbelov.ru
info@arhbelov.ru
Tel +7 (926) 2071121

Mikhail Filippov
-
Lyshchikov pereulok 12 c1,
109240 Moscow

filippovm.ru
info@filippovm.ru
Tel +7 (495) 9153965

Mikhail Khazanov
-
Kozhevnicheskaya ulitsa 10,
115114 Moscow

khazanov-arch.ru
mail@khazanov-arch.ru
Tel +7 (415) 9998931

Mosproekt-2
-
2-ya Brestskaya ulitsa 5,
123056 Moscow

www.mosproject2.ru
info@mosproject2.ru
Tel +7 (499) 2518187

Proekt Meganom
-
Bersnevsky pereulok 5a c1,
119072 Moscow

meganom.moscow
mail@project-meganom.ru
Tel +7 (499) 9510073

Reserve
-
Blagoveshchensky pereulok 3,
123001 Moscow

www.reserve.ru
info@reserve.ru
Tel +7 (495) 7556960

Sergey Gnedovsky
-

www.pnkb.ru
pnkb@list.ru
Tel +7 (495) 6147059

Sergey Kisselev & Partners
-
Shukhova ulitsa 14 c9, 115162 Moscow

www.sk-p.ru
main@sk-p.ru
Tel +7 (495) 6404149

Sergey Skuratov Architects
-
Runovsky pereulok 8 c1, 115184 Moscow

www.skuratov-arch.ru
main@skuratov-arch.ru
Tel +7 (495) 9510735

Sergey Tkatchenko
-
Bolshaya Bronnaya ulitsa 23 c2,
123104 Moscow

www.sbtkachenko.ru
sbt@sbtkachenko.ru
Tel +7 (495) 6516463

SPEECH
-
Krasnoproletarskaya ulitsa 16 c2,
127473 Moscow

www.speech.su
info@speech.su
Tel +7 (495) 7417893

Totan Kuzembaev
-
Lyusinovskaya ulitsa 64 c1, 115162 Moscow

totan.ru
contact@totan.ru
Tel +7 (495) 6693809

Wowhaus Architecture
-
Bersenevsky pereulok 5 c4,
119072 Moscow

wowhaus.ru
anna@wowhaus.ru
Tel +7 (495) 9882094

Remarkable Buildings

02. GUM Department Store
-
Krasnaya ploshchad 3, 101000 Moscow

commercial
A. N. Pomerancev, V. G. Suchov
1890-1893

04. Northern Insurance
-
Ilyinka ulitsa 23, 103132 Moscow

offices
I. Rerberg, V. Oltarzhevsky
1909-1916

05. Mokhovaya residential complex
-
Mokhovaya ulitsa 13, 125009 Moscow

residential
I. Zholtovsky
1932-1934

07. Central Telegraph Office
-
Tverskaya ulitsa 7, 125009 Moscow

offices
I. Rerberg
1927-1929

09. TSUM Department Store
-
Petrovka ulitsa 2, 107031 Moscow

commercial
R. Kleyn
1906-1908

10. Detsky Mir
-
Teatralny prospekt 5, 109012 Moscow

commercial
A. Dushkin, I. Vdovin
1953-1957

11. KGB building
-
Bolshaya Lubyanka ulitsa 2, 101000 Moscow

offices
A. Y. Langman, I. G. Bezrukov
1934

26. Moscow State Academy of Choreography
-
2-ya Frunzenskaya ulitsa 5, 119146 Moscow

educational
V. Lebedev, A. Larin, S. Kusakov
1967-1969

27. Kauchuk Factory Club
-
Plyushchikha ulitsa 64, 119121 Moscow

cultural
K. Melnikov
1927-1929

28. Frunze Military Academy
-
Devichyego Polya proezd 2, 119121 Moscow

educational
L. Rudnev, V. Munts
1932-1937

29. Burdenko residential complex
-
Burdenko ulitsa 9, 119121 Moscow

residential
Sergey Skuratov Architects
2008-2012

31. Ministry of Foreign Affairs
-
Smolenskaya-Sennaya ploshchad 32/34, 119002 Moscow

administrative
V. Gelfreykh, M. Minkus
1949-1952

37. Russian White House
-
Krasnopresnenskaya naberezhnaya 2, 103274 Moscow

governmental
D. Chechulin
1965-1981

38. Sev-Comecon
-
Novy Arbat ulitsa 36, 121205 Moscow

offices
M. Posochin, A. Mndoyants, V. Svirsky
1964-1968

39. Oktyabr Cinema
-
Novy Arbat ulitsa 24, 121069 Moscow

cultural, educational
M. Posokhin, A. Mndojanc,
J. Popov, A. Zdakov, B. Turcinovic
1967

41. Central House of Architects
-
Granatny pereulok 7, 121069 Moscow

offices
A. Burov, A. Vlasov, M. Merzhanov
1939-1940

42. Ryabushinsky Mansion, Gorky Museum
-
Malaya Nikitskaya ulitsa 6/2c5, 121069 Moscow

museum
F. Shekhtel
1900

50. Rossiya Theatre
-
Strastnoy Bulvar 2, 127006 Moscow

theatre
J. Severdjaev, D. Solopov, E. Gadzinskaja
1961

57. Begovaya residential complex
-
Begovaya ulitsa 34, 125284 Moscow

residential
A. Meerson
1978

59. Pravda publishing house
-
Pravdy ulitsa 24c3, 127137 Moscow

offices
P. Golosov
1931-1937

62. Yaroslavsky station
-
Komsomolskaya ploshchad, 107140 Moscow

infrastructure
F. Shekhtel
1902-1904

63. Ex-Garage Novo-Ryazanskaya
-
Novoryazanskaya ulitsa 27, 107078 Moscow

cultural
K. Melnikov, V. Shukhov
1926-1929

65. Ministry of Transport
-
Sadovaya-Spasskaya ulitsa 21, 107078 Moscow

offices, residential
A. Dushkin, B. Mezentsev, V. Abramov
1949-1953

66. NKPS People's Commissariat of Transportation
-
Novaya Basmannaya ulitsa 2/1c1, 107174 Moscow

offices
I. Fomin
1929-1934

67. Gostorg
-
Myasnitskaya ulitsa 47, 101000 Moscow

commercial, offices
B. Velikovsky, M. Barsc, G. Vegman, M. Gaken
1925-27

69. Central Aerohydrodynamic Institute
-
Novokirochny pereulok 2, 105005
Moscow

scientific research
A. Kuznetsov
1924-1926

70. Gazgolder
-
Nizhniy Susalnyy pereulok 5c17,
105064 Moscow

multifunctional
S. Kisselev
2012-2015

73. Military barracks
-
Yauzsky Bulvar 2/16, 109028 Moscow

residential
I. Golosov
1934-1936

75. MOGES-1 electric power plant
-
Raushskaya naberezhnaya 10,
115035 Moscow

industrial
I. Zholtovsky
1927

82. Student dormitory complex
-
Ordzhonikidze ulitsa 8/9,
115419 Moscow

residential
I. Nikolaev
1929

85. Central Dynamo Stadium
-
Moskovskaya alleya, 125167 Moscow

stadium
A. Langman; L. Cherikover
1927-1928; 1933-1934

96. Ostankino Tower
-
Akademika Koroleva ulitsa 15,
129075 Moscow

infrastructural
A. Batalov
1960-1967

97. Monument to the Conquerors of Space
-
Prospekt Mira 111, 129223 Moscow

monument
M. Barsch, A. Kolchin
1964

98. Burevestnik Workers' Club
-
3-ya Rybinskaya ulitsa 17,
107113 Moscow

cultural
K. Melnikov
1927-1929

103. ZiL residential complex
-
Velozavodskaya ulitsa 3/2,
115088 Moscow

residential
I. Milinis
1936-1937

104. ZiL automotive plant
-
Avtozavodskaya ulitsa 23,
115280 Moscow

industrial
E. Popov, V. Vesnin, A. Vesnin
1928-1933

105. Gosplan Garage
-
Aviamotornaya ulitsa 61,
111024 Moscow

garage
K. Melnikov
1936

109. Principal Plaza
-
Oktyabrya prospekt 10, 117312 Moscow

offices
ABD architects
2006-2009

112. Offices on Leninsky Prospekt
-
Udaltsova ulitsa 2, 119415 Moscow

offices
SPEECH
2005-2011

114. Chertanovo Severnoye District
-
Chertanovo Severnoye mkr 5Г,
117303 Moscow

residential
M. Posochin, L. Dyubek, A. Shapiro,
L. Misoznikov, E. Zacharov
1974-1983

115. Yasenevo District
-
Yasnogorskaya ulitsa, 117463 Moscow

residential
Y. Belopolsky, F. Gazevsky, A. Rochegov,
P. Provotorov
1975

116. Nagatino District
-
Nagatinskaya naberezhnaya 1-54,
115470 Moscow

residential
R. Aldonina, P. Zapasov, P. Zamiyatin,
J. Andropov
1974-1984

119. Luzhniki Stadium
-
Luzhniki ulitsa 24, 119048 Moscow

stadium
A. Vlasov, I. Rozhin
1954-1956

120. Young Pioneers Palace
-
Kosygina ulitsa 17к1, 119333 Moscow

cultural
V. Egerev, V. Kubasov, F. Novikov,
B. Paluy, I. Pokrovsky, M. Chazakyan
1959-1962

121. Yugo-Zapadny District
-
Leninsky prospekt 70-72, 119296
Moscow

residential
Y. Belopolsky
1955-1957

122. Troparyovo District
-
Bakinskikh Komissarov ulitsa, 119526
Moscow

residential
A. Bergelson, G. Gavrilov,
V. Korkina, M. Posochin, A. Samsonov
1970

Index by architect

Index by project

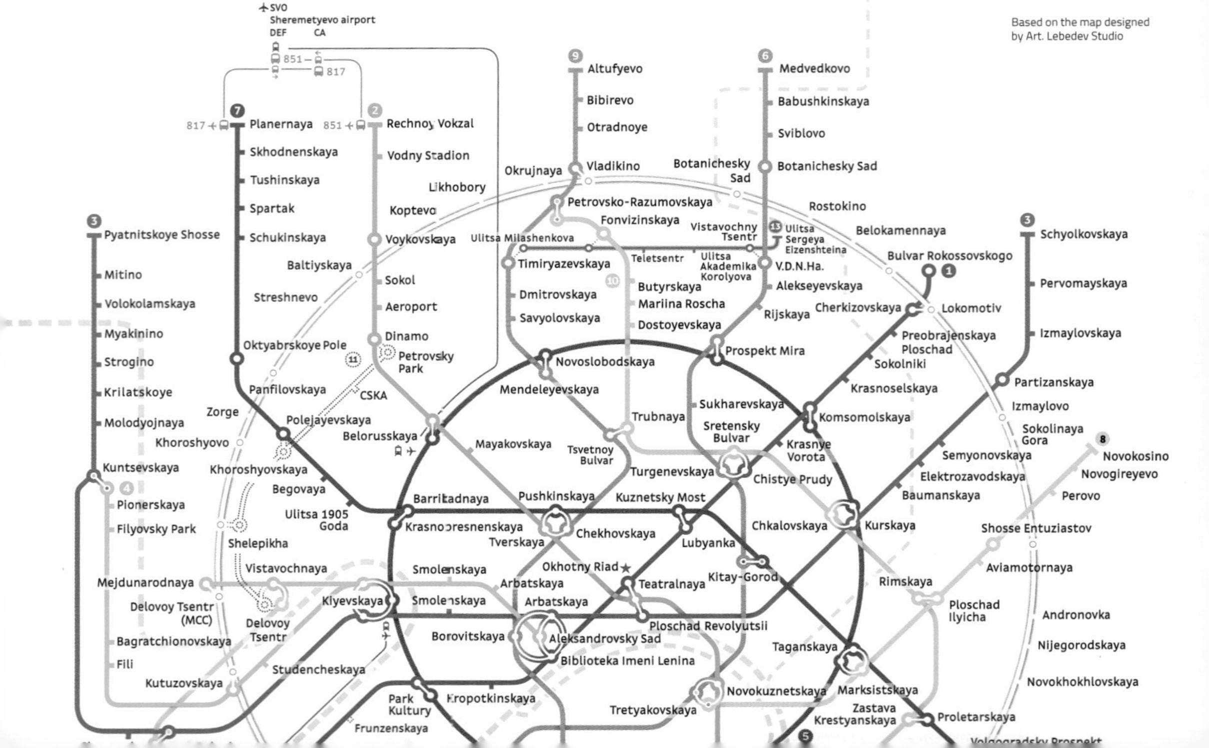

Based on the map designed
by Art. Lebedev Studio